Editorial adviser Professor Asa Briggs
Editor Elizabeth Gundrey

THEN 1901

Then Limited
London

Contents

3 INTRODUCTION
9 FEDERATION IMPERIAL: Australia's great step; Australian immigration.
10 END OF A REIGN: Death of the Queen; Utterly sickened; Passage of the dead Queen; Tributes of laurel leaves; Arrival of the German Emperor; The mourners; Military character.
14 THE RUNABOUT KING: The Queen is dead. Long live the King. Not a dummy.
16 BOER WAR: Negotiations with Botha; Mr. Kruger; The budget; Churchill's maiden speech; The employment of Zulus; European critics; Disgraces and mischiefs; Native races and imperial problems; The army reorganizes; Prudence and honour; The treatment of Boer women and children; The women's camps; Enteric fever rages; 5,000 dead; The church and the camps; Help for the Boers; the blockhouse system in South Africa; Limiting the Boers' mobility; The wrecking of trains; Chamberlain provokes the Germans; German view on camps; Lord Rosebery on Liberal policy and the war; Mr. Asquith at Bilston; The pro-Boer demonstration; The parting of the ways; Little Englanders; South Africa at the year's end; The " Land of Lies "; Foreign criticism; Race hatred.
46 IRISH AND THE CLOSURE: Disgraceful scenes.
48 ENDS OF THE EARTH: The Antarctic expedition; North and South Polar expeditions; A great adventure begins.
51 AN ALLIANCE BAULKED (GERMANY): To stand alone.
52 AFTER THE BOXER RISING: Prince Tuan and the silken-girdle death: the Chinese peace negotiations; The indemnity question; Punishment; Expiation; Reprisals; The Empress Dowager; The Chinese settlement and after; Fleecing the Chinese.
61 RUSSIA IN MANCHURIA: The Manchurian danger; Inability to sign; A Manchurian agreement.
64 AN ALLY AT SEA: A question of size; Balance of naval power in the Far East.
67 THE UNITED STATES—A NEW ALLY: The Hay-Pauncefote treaty signed; Great Britain withdraws.
69 GIANT OF STEEL: Momentous events in the U.S.; £8,000,000 a year profit.
70 ASSASSINATION: The Lynching scene.
74 THE ARTS SCENE.
76 WORKERS STRUGGLE: The Taff Vale case; The status of trade unions; Power to trade unions; Trade unionists react; The new Labour movement.
80 ON THE AIR: Marconi signals across the Atlantic; The telegraphone; the telautograph; Extra-terrestrial communication; Epoch making; Mother Earth's leading strings.
84 THE OPEN ROAD: Record broken; Omnibuses; Race is off; Automobilists united; Military autocars; The horseless carriage; Furiously driving.
87 THREAT FROM THE SEA: The first British submarine; The German Navy.
88 TAKING OFF: Balloon ascent; What is an aeroplane?
89 RAILWAYS FOR NEW MARKETS: The Ugandan railroad; Pax Britannica by rail; Building a twopenny tube.
92 LIFE AND LABOUR: Family Life; A review of Rowntree's book on poverty; New hope; Sunday music in the workhouse.
95 THE CENSUS: Crowded homes make problems for census officials.
98 EDUCATION FOR THE NEW CENTURY: The Government Education Bill; Educate for industry; The Cockerton judgement; Child labour.
101 THE NEW WOMAN: The duel of sex; Lady surgeon will not resign; Women and the legal profession; Women, labour and their wages; Women's International Progressive Union; Women's Trade Union League; Brief, bright and sisterly; A lady publisher.
105 MISCELLANY.

Introduction

On the night of 31 December 1900 a violent gale blew over many parts of Britain, violent enough to bring down one of the upright stones at Stonehenge. To some people it seemed a fitting end for an old century. To other people the century had already ended a year earlier, and not all of these were convinced to the contrary by the Astronomer Royal's scientific assurance that since numbering begins as 1, not 0, the first day of January 1901 really did mark the beginning of something new.

Yet before more than a few weeks were out there was no doubt that the old was giving way to the new. Queen Victoria died at Osborne, Isle of Wight, on 22 January, surrounded by her many children and grandchildren, including the Emperor of Germany. It was difficult at the time to do justice to what had happened. " What a series of changes political and social this event will produce ! " Lord Esher noted in his Journal the day Edward VII ascended to the throne. " It is like beginning to live again in a new world. "

This was a widely shared opinion inside and outside Court circles, since Victoria, who had given her name to an ism *as well as to an age, had been present, if not always at the centre of the scene, through all the changing circumstances of sixty-three years of more rapid and far-reaching change than the world had ever known. The* Annual Register *reporting her death chose a longer time span for its perspective. " The feeling of forlornness which pervaded the country was, alike in its diffusion and depth, of a kind such as had not been known since the death of King Alfred a thousand years before. "*

No one could say authoritatively what that earlier feeling had been, although a few journalists, writing for new large-circulation newspapers, had a good try. Later in the year, indeed, there were to be stirring commemorations in Winchester and elsewhere of the millenary of Alfred's death, and for once Lord

Rosebery was to abandon the Boer War and " national efficiency " as speech-making themes and deliver a " striking address " on the life and character of " that great monarch ".

What was not new in 1901 was the poverty beneath the surface, though it was being revealed to the nation in new ways. Rowntree's Poverty, A Study of Town Life, *a new book of the year, showed that the extent of poverty in an ancient cathedral city in the north of England was as shocking as that in Charles Booth's London. Moreover, the Boer War itself exposed every kind of social weakness in Britain—malnutrition, physical unfitness, ignorance. In Manchester alone, to take an example which was soon to be much publicised, 8,000 out of 11,000 would-be volunteers for the War had to be turned away and of the remainder 2,000 were fit only for the militia. The demand for " national efficiency " was to gain strength from the publication of such statistics: so, though more slowly and in face of greater resistance, was the demand for radical social reform.*

There were few signs in 1901 that questions of social policy would loom large at the end of the decade, although nearly every proposal which was to be effected then had already been mooted. The Chancellor of the Exchequer in his budget speech had to deal with the thorny question of protective tariffs—and he dealt with it very warily—but he had no need to dwell on welfare. One of the most memorable passages in his budget speech was that revenues from beer duties had fallen during the previous year, due " possibly to a diminished spending power and to the absence of so many beer consumers in South Africa ".

The Census figures of 1901 are more interesting than the budget figures. The size of middle-class families had begun to fall—the average was now four children—while the size of labourers' families remained high—an average of six children. There were enormous variations in infant mortality, in occupational mortality, in heights and weights of schoolchildren, in consumption of meat and milk and sugar. There were picturesque contrasts in clothes and in ways of life between class and class, contrasts which were sharpening. At the base of the pyramid, village labourers were not only badly off but could expect little or nothing from the future: their weekly wages varied from twelve shillings a week in Oxfordshire to one pound in County Durham. Much was to be made of all these vital and social statistics before the decade was out, but almost the only piece of social legislation of the year, the Factory Act, was a measure merely consolidating and codifying the laws of the previous century rather than anticipating the policies of the twentieth century.

Leisure activities sometimes brought people together from different social groups, but there were big social differences here too. There were 114,000 people at the F.A. Cup Final at the Crystal Palace ground watching a drawn match between Tottenham Hotspur and Sheffield United—the largest crowd ever. (Tottenham won the replay at Bolton.) Yet all sports had sharp distinctions between " amateurs " and " professionals ". You had far more leisure if you had lots of domestic servants, as many people did, but usually very little if you actually were a domestic servant, as one-and-a-half million out of the four million women then employed were. Ostentation and drudgery went together. The day began with the lighting of the kitchen fire, if you had the money to buy the coal. It might end in the theatre, the music hall—there were fifty of them in London—or the public house. Vast amounts were spent on liquor—and gambling—by all classes. Whisky cost between 3s. and 5s. 6d. a bottle, and the Chancellor believed that the limit on profitable taxation had now been reached.

There were almost as many variations between one part of the country and another as there were between one class and another. Indeed, the two kinds of difference were related to each other. In Hampstead there were eighty women domestics to every hundred house-occupiers: in Rochdale there were seven. In Liverpool and Coventry most houses had water-closets; in Blackburn and Wigan fewer than half. Religious differences were also highly localised. The relative pull of Church and Chapel still depended very much on where you were brought up. The Nonconformists were to be aroused the following year in rebellion against the Unionist Government's Education Bill: in 1901 they included the fiercest spokesmen of temperance and the staunchest critics of the Boer War. In London two out of eleven people were still attending a place of worship on Sundays. In Oxford and Cambridge " there were pockets of militant atheism ", but, in the words of G. M. Young, the historian, who was in his early undergraduate days, " to be blatantly irreligious was not good form ".

Young has also said of this period that while there was plenty to read and to argue about—Shaw's plays, Wells's novels, Chesterton's essays, Hardy's poems—the balance between old and new had not yet been settled. The outer fabric of life remained what it had been despite the emergence of new social and economic forces, despite the rise of science. The motor car was still a toy, though rather less of a toy than it had been, and the aeroplane was a fairy tale. Submarines were becoming a reality, although even Wells, prophet of education and of technology, had refused to believe that submarines of any variety could do more than suffocate their inventors and their crews out at sea. There were visions in 1901 of French soldiers in baggy blue breeches landing off submarines near Eastbourne and marching on London. The nightmares of German invaders came later.

The Boer War had revealed Britain's isolation in Europe, but there still seemed to be an imperial future. Curzon in India was sure of it, and one of Queen Victoria's last public acts was to send a message of congratulation to the new Governor-General of Australia wishing the new Commonwealth and all her beloved subjects there prosperity and well-being. The year ended with the Christian socialist, Scott Holland, arguing that whatever else might happen overseas the traditional figure of John Bull was obsolete. " In the first place, he is fat; and the fat man's day is past and gone. . . . Over the wide horizons of the Empire, the fat men have all disappeared . . . In their place is the long lean Australian, so curiously American in the type that he runs to. He is tall and compact, bony and muscular. And your African colonist follows suit."

Scott Holland was no more right about America than Curzon was about India. It was difficult in 1901 for most Englishmen to understand other people in other parts of the world. McKinley's last words after his assassination by a small dark immigrant were: " Goodbye all, goodbye ! It is God's way. His will be done." The words were clearer to understand than the meaning of what had happened. There was little point, a British meteorologist told his fellow-countrymen during the year, in exchanging the climate of England for Continental and other resorts. " The English climate is the most healthy one in the world, and the death rate of the health resorts to which English people betake themselves is higher than London, and much higher than the country districts of the British Isles." Edward VII was not to treat such a point of view too seriously. But then, he was willing to move at a different pace from that of many Englishmen. It was thought noteworthy enough to report in July that he had travelled from Marlborough House to Windsor Castle in his motor-car in " about an hour ".

Asa Briggs

THE SPIRIT OF PUNCH "HIC ET UBIQUE."

PARTNERS.

Britannia. "AFTER ALL, MY DEAR, WE NEEDN'T TROUBLE OURSELVES ABOUT THE OTHERS."
Colonia. "NO; WE CAN ALWAYS DANCE TOGETHER, YOU AND I!"

Punch

FEDERATION IMPERIAL

Federation came late to Australia because each of the six colonies was thousands of miles from the others. But with the coming of the railways, they had closer contact; and the wish for a national rail system was one factor in the urge to federate.

Australia's Great Step

Daily Express, 2 January.

To judge by the way in which some pessimistic statesmen are wont to speak of the British Empire, one might suppose it to be an aged and decrepit thing. As a matter of fact, it has not yet reached the heyday of its youth. The dangers and the rocks ahead, on which they who mistrust the strong Imperialist fervour of to-day are prone to dilate, belong, at any rate, to the period of lusty youth rather than worn-out old age. The Empire is in no more advanced a state than that of formation. The great chain is but being forged, and it was literally only yesterday that one of the links was completed by the setting-up of the Commonwealth of Australia.

The vast importance of the step which has just been taken by Australia has perhaps been scarcely realised as it deserves in the Mother-Country. The war in South Africa, the startling and humiliating discovery of our state of military unpreparedness—these and other scarcely less engrossing matters have not allowed us to concentrate our attention on the event proceeding in Australia as we should surely have done at a less anxious time in our history. We have watched with sympathy, but not with the wonder and enthusiasm we might well have felt and shown. Perhaps even Australia has not been aroused through her length and breadth as might have been expected. Yet this is not saying that the new Commonwealth has been still-born. On the contrary, at Sydney and elsewhere there were rejoicings and celebrations yesterday on a great scale. And it is very significant of the entirely loyal and patriotic temper of the Australians that, in celebrating their own step upward on the ladder of nations, they have not forgotten Motherland and Mother Queen.

The Federation of the Empire has long been talked and written of in Great Britain; but it is from Greater Britain, apparently, that we must look for real progress. We in the Mother-Country may have suggested Canadian Federation, but it was Canada herself who proved it possible; and now Australia has acted on her own initiative. The federating of Australia is an experiment, and the minds who have conceived the idea and carried it out would not affect to be infallible. If it were to fail, then those who had been longing and working for the close union of all parts of a yet inchoate Empire might well feel that their cause had received a grievous setback. But if it succeeds and works well—as we firmly believe it will—then assuredly we shall have a splendid object lesson, illustrating the practicability and the desirableness of Imperial Federation.

Left: Britain still believed that her Empire made her independent of European ties. But behind-scenes diplomacy was already bringing to an end the policy of isolation.

Australian Immigration

The Times, 9 August.

Strong objection is being taken to the educational test which it is proposed to insert in the Immigration Bill, by which every immigrant is required to write 50 words of English dictated by an immigration officer. The Labour members consider the Bill too mild, and intend proposing amendments directly aimed against coloured races, including the Japanese.

End of a Reign

Although she had lived withdrawn from public life, Victoria's character and the great events of her reign had had a world-wide impact. Her family connexions spread through most of the still-flourishing monarchies of Europe. Mourning was international.

Death of The Queen. The Last Hours at Osborne.

The Times, 23 January.

All day long the Angel of Death has been hovering over Osborne House. One could almost hear the beating of his wings, but at half-past 6 those wings were folded, and the Queen was at rest. To those who knew her Majesty best and most closely, as some of them have told me, the whole event seems incredible and unreal. To all of them the life of the Queen has seemed a part of the natural order of things, a thing as certain as the rising or the setting of the sun; and they are simply incapable of realizing what it means, and that feeling will be shared by almost all of those who were the Queen's subjects, but are now the subjects of him who was the Prince of Wales, and to whom no new title is likely to be generally applied until after the Queen's funeral. Foreseen and expected as the event has been, it is a shock now that it has actually come; and the effect of it has been to cause a feeling of stunned bewilderment, which seems for the present to drown all expressions of grief. Not that Osborne House is not full of sorrowful hearts, from the heart of the German Emperor, whose coming has been a real comfort to the Royal Family, to that of the simplest servant in the house. That feeling will extend over the country, and it certainly is felt by me in such measure as to render the task of writing very difficult indeed. The Queen is gone from her people

Graphic

One of the last portraits of the Queen.

full of years and honour. Their loss is irreparable, but they may take some comfort from the thought that for her the beautiful prayer of Tennyson has been exactly fulfilled. That which he wrote, in dedicating the *Idylls of the King* to the dead Prince Consort, in an address to the Queen, was:

May all love,
His love unseen, but felt, o'ershadow
Thee,
The love of all Thy sons encompass Thee,
The love of all Thy daughters
cherish Thee,
The love of all Thy people comfort Thee,
Till God's love set Thee at His side again.

All this might now be written with abundant and full truth in the past sense of a Queen without stain or reproach, who has passed away full of years and honour.

Utterly Sickened

Letter from Henry James.

Reform Club,
Pall Mall, S.W.
January 22, 1901.

Blind, used up, utterly sickened and humiliated by the War, which she hated and deplored from the first (it's what has finished her) and by the way everything is going, she is a very pathetic old monarchial figure. She had been failing fast for days before it became public, and was far gone when the first news of her being ill came. It is a simple running down of this old used up watch—and no winding up can keep her for more than from hour to hour. . . .

I feel as if her death will have consequences in and for this country that no man can foresee. The Prince of Wales is an arch-vulgarian (don't repeat this from me); the wretched little ' Yorks ' [*later, George V and Queen Mary*] are less than nothing; the Queen's magnificent duration had held all things magnificently — beneficiently — together and prevented all sorts of accidents. Her death, in short, will let loose incalculable forces for possible ill. I am very pessimistic. The Prince of Wales, in sight of the throne, and nearly 60, and after all he has done besides of the same sort, is ' carrying on ' with Mrs. George Keppel in a manner of the worst men for the dignity of things. His succession, in short, is ugly and makes for all vulgarity and frivolity.

RTHPL

Royal mourners (see page 12) follow on foot the last stage of the coffin's journey from Windsor to the royal mausoleum.

Passage of the Dead Queen from Osborne, Isle of Wight, to Portsmouth

Letter from Countess of Denbigh.

Slowly down the long line of battleships came eight white Torpedo destroyers, dark gliding forms, and after them the white *Alberta* looking very small and frail next to the towering battleships. We could see the motionless figures standing round the white pall which, with the crown and orb and sceptre, lay upon the coffin. Solemnly and slowly, it glided over the calm blue water, followed by the other three vessels, giving one a strange choke, and a catch in one's heart as memory flew back to her triumphal passage down her fleet in the last Jubilee review. As slowly and silently as it came the cortège passed away into the haze: with the solemn booming of the guns continuing every minute till Portsmouth was reached.

Tributes of Laurel Leaves

The whole nation was deeply moved by the death of the monarch, and joined in those extravagant mourning rites so beloved of the Victorians.

The Times, 2 February.

Outside the station, in Buckingham Palace Road, the first objects that attract the eye are the dark green wreaths suspended from the lamp posts. This happy idea originated with Miss Etta Close, of 101 Eaton Square. Having obtained the permission of the local authorities to carry out her scheme of decoration, Miss Close formed a committee of ladies, and issued an appeal for wreaths. The response to the appeal has been most remarkable. By Wednesday night garlands more than sufficient for the 800 lamps along the line of route were received, and they were hung up early yesterday morning.

Arrival of the German Emperor

Graphic, 26 January.

There can be no doubt as to the affection and reverence felt by Emperor William for his English grandmother. It was no slight feeling which led the Emperor to break off the important festivities in honour of the Prussian bi-centenary and to leave his capital at a moment's notice. "I am Her Majesty's eldest grandson," he is reported to have said, "and my mother is unable from illness to hasten to her bedside." Directly His Majesty heard the bad news he decided to come, a special train was kept with steam up, and as soon as he could despatch his State business the Emperor hurried off with the Duke of Connaught, attended by the smallest of suites. So prompt was his departure that although the British Admiralty sent off the British Cruiser *Minerva* to bring him across she could not arrive in time, and the Emperor hastily chartered an ordinary Flushing mail steamer, the *Engeland.*

The Mourners

Royal relatives from the great houses of Europe followed the Queen's coffin.

Graphic, 9 February.

The King, who was in the uniform of a Field-Marshal, covered with a dark cloak, walked alone. He was followed by the German Emperor, whose attitude throughout the ceremonies has appealed strongly to the public imagination, the Duke of Connaught, the King of Portugal, and other Royal princes. Then came the Queen and other Royal ladies, all in deep mourning and thickly veiled. Her Majesty, who attracted the keenest and most sympathetic attention, led by the hand her little grandson, Prince Edward, who was dressed in sailor costume. The King and his party stood outside the entrance to the chapel, and there was a brief interval of silence, broken only by the solemn tolling of bells and the boom of the minute-gun, fired some distance away in the grounds by a battery of artillery. At three o'clock punctually the coffin was slowly borne out of the chapel and placed reverently upon the gun-carriage, after which the pall, with the crown and other emblems of Sovereignty, as before, were placed upon the coffin.

The following was the order of the procession:

The Queen's Company of Grenadier Guards, with reversed arms.
Highland Pipers.
Royal Servants.
Band of the Grenadier Guards.
The Bishop of Winchester.
The Dean of Windsor.
The Lord Chamberlain.
The Lord Steward.

THE GUN-CARRIAGE
Supported by Her Late Majesty's Equerries and Household

THE KING
The German Emperor
The King of the Belgians
The King of Portugal
The Duke of Connaught
Prince Henry of Prussia
Prince Christian of Schleswig-Holstein
Prince Arthur of Connaught
The Duke of Saxe-Coburg and Gotha
The Grand Duke of Hesse
The Crown Prince of Germany
Prince Albert of Schleswig-Holstein
Prince Alexander of Battenberg
Prince Louis of Battenberg
Prince Adolph of Schaumburg-Lippe

Military Character

Keir Hardie, the first Labour M.P., used the funeral arrangements as a stick with which to beat the government.

The Times, 26 March.

Mr. Keir Hardie (Merthyr Tydvil) objected to the mourning stationery supplied to the House of Commons in connexion with the death of Queen Victoria. Its hideous black border was offensive to the eye and the taste. (Ministerial laughter.) If hon. gentlemen opposite had no taste he could not help it.

The Speaker.—Order, order. The hon. gentleman must not make these irregular remarks.

Mr. Keir Hardie.—I wish to say, Sir, that hon. gentlemen sitting opposite are evidently not in a condition to behave themselves.

Mansell

Above: One of the last family gatherings at Osborne House, Isle of Wight. The Queen is surrounded by British and German princes and princesses, dukes and duchesses and, on Victoria's left, the beautiful Queen of Spain.

The Speaker.—Order, order. That again is an irregular observation, and I must ask the hon. gentleman to withdraw it.

Mr. Keir Hardie.—He desired also to enter a most emphatic protest against the military character of the funeral of the late Queen to the total exclusion of any representation of the civil or religious life of the community. (Hear, hear.) The leading characteristic of the late Queen was domestic simplicity. It seemed to him a mockery that the last ceremony in connexion with the passing of such a Queen should be a huge military procession from which all feelings of reverence were excluded. (Ministerial cries of " No.") What he felt then, and what he felt now, was that the dead body of England's Queen was being used as a recruiting sergeant to help the military designs now being carried into effect. (Cries of " Oh.")

Below: Military pomp in the procession through London provoked some criticism that the Queen's funeral was being exploited as a large-scale and tasteless recruiting display for the Boer War.

RTHPL

The Runabout King

Edward VII opened up the Court to businessmen and to pretty women, and enlivened it with balls and banquets. Fond of travel, he did much to improve Britain's relations with France and other countries. To the Kaiser he was "a satan," to his people (in a popular song):

He's the monarch to make things hum,
The King, the runabout King!

The Queen is dead Long live the King

The Times, 23 January.

The Throne is never vacant, and at the very moment of parting from our Queen we turn to acclaim our King. He must at once take the oath as Sovereign and will preside at a meeting of the Council, and this very afternoon Parliament, hurriedly summoned, will assemble to swear allegiance to the new monarch. He whom we have so long known as the Prince of Wales, and who has won for that title the affectionate regard of the country, now claims its homage as its rightful King. He enters upon a great heritage of loyalty to the Throne established by his mother's long and beneficent reign, and he may count with certainty upon its transference to himself. The King has undergone a long training in the best of schools and has proved himself the possessor of great natural aptitudes for the duties of Royalty, of which no inconsiderable share has fallen to his lot to discharge for many years past. Indeed, so great has been the part he has played in the State as Prince of Wales that, on ascending the Throne in his sixtieth year, he will exercise, at least in the

Edward VII, an early enthusiast for motoring, with the future Lord Montagu of Beaulieu.

RTHPL

ceremonial sphere, functions with which he is scarcely less familiar than if their actual discharge had been his for the ordinary lifetime of a generation. Endowed as he is with many of the most lovable and attractive qualities of his mother—with warm sympathies, with a kind heart, with a generous disposition, and with a quick appreciation of genuine worth—the nation is happy in the confidence that in spirit as well as in form it may count upon the maintenance of that conception of Royalty which is the only one that most of us have ever known. To these qualities the King adds perfect tact, wide knowledge of men, and the business virtues of method, prompt decision, punctuality, and great capacity for work.

There is no position in the world more difficult to fill than that of Heir Apparent to the Throne. It is beset by more than all the temptations of actual Royalty, while the weight of counteracting responsibility is much less directly felt. It must be with a feeling akin to hopelessness that a man in that position offers up the familiar prayer, " Lead us not into temptation."

RTHPL

Edward VII was 60 when he came to the throne, because his mother refused to abdicate in his favour.

Not a dummy

Letter from Conan Doyle to his mother, March.

He asked that I should be placed next to him. He proved an able, clearheaded, positive man, rather inclined to be noisy, very alert, and energetic. He won't be a dummy king. He will live to be about seventy, I should say.

Will he change?

Letter from Winston Churchill (in Canada) to his mother, 22 January.

My dearest Mamma,

So the Queen is dead. The news reached us at Winnipeg and this city far away among the snows—fourteen hundred miles from any British town of importance—began to hang its head and hoist half-masted flags. A great and solemn event: but I am curious to know about the King. Will it entirely revolutionise his way of life? Will he sell his horses and scatter his Jews or will Reuben Sassoon be enshrined among the crown jewels and other regalia? Will he become desperately serious? Will he continue to be friendly to you? Will the Keppel* be appointed 1st Lady of the Bedchamber?

* *Mrs. Keppel, Edward VII's mistress.*

THE BOER WAR

British policy in South Africa was for ultimate self-government, and equality of Africans before the law. Some Dutch (Boer) settlers disliked this and attempted to found breakaway republics with their own laws (e.g. slavery permitted). They established two, the Transvaal and the Orange Free State.

When gold was found in the former, so many Britons went there (the "uitlanders") that they soon outnumbered the Boers, who taxed them heavily but denied them a vote. Britain therefore sought to annex the Transvaal and this led to war in 1899.

At first, the Boers gained the upper hand, invading British territory and besieging towns; but in 1900 Britain succeeded in annexing the Transvaal. Guerilla warfare continued, however, with the Boer army wearing civilian clothes and using commando tactics.

In 1901, there was an abortive attempt at a settlement. Meanwhile, many Boer farmers pledged themselves not to aid the commandos and in return were left alone by the British army, but were then likely to have their farms and crops burned by the commandos, and their families left homeless. The British took these women and children into camps, which soon became the centre of infectious diseases that killed tens of thousands.

To impede the commandos, the British then criss-crossed the farmlands with a system of blockhouses and barbed wire. They began executions in the field, and started enlisting black Africans. These methods, and the state of the women's camps, provoked sharp protest in Britain, led by the social worker, Emily Hobhouse.

Who was who? *Milner: Britain's High Commissioner in South Africa. Kruger: President of the Transvaal. Kitchener: Britain's Commander-in-Chief there. French, Haig: British generals. Botha: the Boer Commandant-General. De Wet, Hertzog, Smuts: Boer generals. Joseph Chamberlain: Britain's Colonial Secretary. Emily Hobhouse: social worker and campaigner for peace in South Africa, who obtained permission to visit and report on the women's camps. Brodrick: Secretary for War.*

NEGOTIATIONS

The British attempts to end the war, even though accompanied by offers of generous indemnity, met with rejection. The fighting dragged on into 1902 before the Boers would admit defeat.

The Negotiations with Botha

The Times, 8 April.

The last monthly bulletin of the " French Africa Committee " contains an article relative to the recent negotiations between Lord Kitchener and Louis Botha, which is worth reproducing, because this bulletin endeavours to judge men and things with the desire not to act on mere bias.

Evidently the Boers are not in agreement one with another, and the letter in which Botha brought the negotiations to an end proves that he neither undertook them nor continued them sincerely, and that their failure, far from being due to Mr. Chamberlain, Lord Kitchener, or Sir A. Milner, was foreseen and calculated. The sole object was to gain time, and to show to the world that the Republicans are resolved to pursue the struggle and to make it drag on as long as possible, because in one way or another they are encouraged to continue it, having been made to think that by so doing they will finally force England to give up the contest and acknowledge their independence as she was forced to do in the case of the United States. Conditions offered by the English were such as the Boers could accept.

The British Government agreed to pay the requisitions made by the Governments of the two Republics and to indemnify the inhabitants. The restriction of the amount to £1,000,000 should not have frightened the burghers, since this sum, it is said, is more than enough to cover the requisitions of the Transvaal and Orange Free State.

" But by a careful perusal of the British conditions plausible enough explanations may be found of the rupture. In the first place, the Boers hoped, perhaps, that by surrendering they would obtain some degree of autonomy, and not a military administration to be succeeded by the *régime* of Crown Colony. Moreover, as may be seen, if Mr. Chamberlain consented to an amnesty for the burghers of the two Republics he did not do the same for the Cape and Natal Afrikanders. To be sure, he did not manifest the intention of forcing them to return to the colonies, but, as a matter of fact, he reduced them to the state of banished persons, since he stipulated that if the rebel Afrikanders returned home they would be subject to the laws of those colonies created especially as a consequence of the war—that is to say, to martial law. The loyalty of the Boers, the close fellowship of arms which has grown up between them and the Afrikanders during so many combats in common may very well have rendered this clause odious to them.

Graphic

In March, General Botha rode to Middelburg to discuss a possible truce.

There is another clause that cannot have pleased them and must have seemed to them somewhat unexpected. The English have burned their farms, and the Boers thus ruined asked the conqueror for means to reconstruct them. Now Mr. Chamberlain replies that measures would be devised to help them by means of loans. That is to say, the British Government, not content with having politically conquered their country, would become their creditor and take a mortgage on their private property. Perhaps this was enough to drive to an obstinate resistance men who are so inveterately enamoured of their personal liberty as well as of their political independence. . . ."

Kruger's Decline

The Times, 19 December.

An Edinburgh telegram states that an influential Transvaal lady, who has just returned to this country from visiting Mr. Kruger, states that she found him in a condition of senile decay and employing a great part of the time of his secretary in writing out texts of Scripture.

The Budget Reflects the Increasing Burden of the War

The Times, 31 December.

The estimates were swollen not only by the actual cost of the war, but by the sums required to meet the public demand for increased armaments, both military and naval. These " ordinary " estimates, which were almost exactly double the ordinary estimates of ten or fifteen years ago, amounted to £61,000,000, while the " extraordinary " war charges for the year were put down provisionally at about the same sum. The Chancellor of the Exchequer, therefore, though the revenue actually exceeded the estimate, found himself face to face with a deficit of £55,000,000. About a quarter of this he proposed to meet by additional taxation and by suspending the Sinking Fund; the rest, some £41,000,000, was to be raised by loan, authority for which was in due course granted by the House. The new taxes were the raising of the income-tax to 1s. 2d., a duty of 4s. 2d. per cwt. on sugar, and of 1s. per ton on exported coal.

The British public became a restless mount for Joseph Chamberlain, whose imperial fervour for the Boer War was not shared by all as it became burdensome at home.

The Colonial Secretary: Confound the brute; I believe he's going to shy again. These blinkers are no good after all. I only hope he won't turn round, or I believe I shall fall off.

Morning Leader

Winston Churchill's Maiden Speech

18 February.

I do not propose to discuss the ethics of farm burning now; but hon. Members should, I think, cast their eyes back to the fact that no considerations of humanity prevented the German army from throwing its shells into dwelling houses in Paris, and starving the inhabitants of that great city to the extent that they had to live upon rats and like atrocious foods in order to compel the garrison to surrender. I venture to think His Majesty's Government would not have been justified in restricting their commanders in the field from any methods of warfare which are justified by precedents set by European and American generals during the last fifty or sixty years. I do not agree very fully with the charges of treachery on the one side and barbarity on the other. From what I saw of the war—and I sometimes saw something of it—I believe that as compared with other wars, especially those in which a civil population took part, this war in South Africa has been on the whole carried on with unusual humanity.

I invite the House to consider which form of government—civil government or military government—is most likely to be conducive to the restoration of the banished prosperity of the country and most likely to encourage the return of the population now scattered far and wide. I understand that there are hon. Members who are in hopes that representative institutions may directly follow military government, but I think they cannot realise thoroughly how very irksome such military government is. I have the greatest respect for British officers, and when I hear them attacked, as some hon. Members have done in their speeches, it makes me very sorry, and very angry too. Although I regard British officers in the field of war, and in dealing with native races, as the best officers in the world, I do not believe that either their training or their habits of thought qualify them to exercise arbitrary authority over civil populations of European race. I have often myself been very much ashamed to see respectable old Boer farmers—the Boer is a curious combination of the squire and the peasant, and under the rough coat of the farmer there are very often to be found the instincts of the squire—I have been ashamed to see such men ordered about peremptorily by young subaltern officers, as if they were private soldiers. I do not hesitate to say that as long as you have anything like direct military government there will be no revival of trade, no return of the Uitlander population, no influx of immigrants from other parts of the world—nothing but despair and discontent on the part of the Boer population, and growing resentment on the part of our own British settlers.

Some hon. Members have seen fit, either in this place or elsewhere, to stigmatise this war as a war of greed. I regret that I feel bound to repudiate that pleasant suggestion. If there were persons who rejoiced in this war, and went out with hopes of excitement or the lust of conflict, they have had enough and more than enough to-day. If, as the hon. Member for Northampton [*Henry Labouchere, Liberal*] has several times suggested, certain capitalists spent money in bringing on this war in the hope that it would increase the value of their mining properties, they know now that they made an uncommonly bad bargain. With the mass of the nation, with the whole people of the country, this war from beginning to end has only been a war of duty. They believe, and they have shown in the most remarkable manner that they believe, that His Majesty's Government and the Colonial Secretary have throughout been actuated by the same high and patriotic motives.

Hope for Distinction

19 February.

Mr. Asquith: My honourable friend the junior Member for Oldham—whose interesting and eloquent speech last night we must all hope and believe, and especially those of us who, like myself, enjoyed the privilege of friendship with his illustrious father, was the first step in a Parliamentary career of the highest distinction.

THE BLACK AFRICANS

The general attitude of fear and distaste at the prospect of employing black Africans to fight, or to give close support to troops, clashed with expediency.

The Employment of Zulus

The Times, 18 May.

Mr. Brunner, member of the Natal Legislative Assembly for the Eshowe District, writes as follows to the *Natal Mercury*:—

" Steps have been taken with the cognisance of the highest military authorities in the country to let loose the natives upon the already demoralized enemy, permission being given to them to loot and plunder. The natives of Zululand have been instructed by the military officers to arm and invade the Vryheid districts. Thousands of head of Boer cattle were brought in and handed over to Colonel Bottomley, and the Zulus were allowed 10 per cent. of all the plunder. One Boer, Cornelius Muller, has been seriously wounded with assegais. As a result of this action the Dinizulu and Usibepu tribes are again on the war path."

Mr. Brunner also publishes a telegram of protest sent to the Premier of Natal, and what is stated to be the latter's reply, to the effect that he had sent protest after protest to the military authorities, but that he believed that Colonel Bottomley had greatly exceeded the instructions given in the original order.

European Critics

The Times, 5 August.

Mr. Chamberlain's speech and ex-President Kruger's statement to the representative of the *Figaro* have revived the discussion of South African affairs in the Austrian Press. That certain organs should again accuse England of waging a war of extermination is only what was to be expected. But even moderate journals comment unfavourably upon the employment of natives, which some of them represent as a breach of the law of nations. They also express fears of the consequences of the harsher measures which are understood to be contemplated. It is announced from Brussels that the Boer executive committee will resort to the severest reprisals, including the shooting of all prisoners.

' Disgraces and Mischiefs '

The Times, 16 August [Parliamentary report].

Sir W. Harcourt (Monmouthshire, W.) said, " Unless we are mistaken in all the reports that have reached us through the Press, the hope of resistance by military operations seems to have been given up in despair, and we are to enter upon a new policy. I hope it is not the policy which the Colonial Secretary the other day dealt with, a most dangerous policy, I thought—I mean the policy of employing savage races and native forces. I hope not, but he made a sort of general defence, as I understood, of the employment of savages in warfare. A greater crime than warfare of that description it is impossible to describe. Of all that is recorded against this country in the unhappy contest with the people of America none left such a stain upon the Administration as that. I hope, if there is any question of employing savages in warfare between white races such as that in which we are now engaged, that the language of Lord Chatham will be remembered. He said ' My lords, who is the man that, in addition to these disgraces and mischiefs to our Army, has dared to authorize, and to associate with our arms, the tomahawk and scalping-knife of the savage, to call into civilized alliance the wild and inhuman savage of the woods, to delegate to the merciless Indian the defence of disputed rights, and to wage the horrors of his barbarous war against our brethren? My lords, these enormities cry aloud to us to redress and avenge them. Unless thoroughly done away with it will be a stain on the national character; it is a violation of the Constitution; I believe it is against law.' I do not wish to be understood as charging or even suggesting that this is the policy which the Government contemplate. But it is perfectly certain that in the Press of this country it has been and is advocated. Language was used not many days ago by the Colonial Secretary to the effect that he saw no reason why native races should not be employed for this purpose. I hope he will entirely disavow any suggestion of the kind."

Native Races as Imperial Problems

The Natives of South Africa; Their Economic and Social Condition. Edited by the South African Native Races Committee. *Nature, 27 May: a review.*

The importance as well as the difficulty of the problems involved is evident. The total native population is estimated by the editors at about five times the numerical strength of that of the whites, and it is rapidly increasing. The natives are not allowed to indulge as they once did in intertribal wars, which would not only give them occupation but keep down their numbers. They are not at present fit for continuous labour. The habit of work is a growth of civilisation, and cannot be imposed as you put a coat of paint on a door. Generations are required to raise a people from savagery. It is no wonder, therefore, that the increase of their numbers and their idleness are sources of anxiety to the intrusive colonists. Various expedients have been tried. The Boer policy was first massacre, then slavery, cruelty and oppression. Nor have our own people always been guiltless in this respect. The results have been lamentable alike to the natives and to the Europeans. With the abolition of slavery a more humane policy on the part of the Government was inaugurated. But neither the Home Government nor the Colonial Governments have been invariably wise or consistent. Though on the whole their efforts have been honestly directed to the benefit of the natives, the conflicting interests of natives and colonists have often caused, and still cause, grave difficulties. The experiment has been made in Cape Colony and, to a more limited extent, in Natal, where the native question is more acute, of admitting natives who fulfil certain stringent conditions to the franchise. The numbers admitted are not yet large, but it is obvious that the principle thus introduced may involve consequences which cannot at present be foreseen.

CLEAN UP THE WAR OFFICE

Even after Lord Roberts became Commander-in-Chief of the Army, important parts of its functions (such as training) were out of his control, and in the hands of junior officers of the Adjutant General. The cavalry were short of horses, the infantry of men, and the artillery of ammunition.

The Army Reorganizes

The Times, 31 December.

From the moment of Lord Roberts's return at the beginning of the year to take up the position of Commander-in-Chief, questions of Army reform, of the organization of the War Office and of military expenditure, have naturally held a prominent place in the national councils. Before speaking of them, however, we may mention that one of the last public acts of Queen Victoria was to receive Lord Roberts at Osborne, and to confer on him an Earldom and the Garter. A Parliamentary vote of £100,000 followed in due course. As to the reforms, the first step was the appointment of a strong Committee of inquiry into the work of the War Office, the chairman of which was Mr. Clinton Dawkins, formerly Finance Minister in Egypt and India. The very valuable Report of this Committee was issued in the early summer, and has to a certain extent been acted upon by Mr. Brodrick [*War Minister*]. Earlier in the year, on March 4, some sensation was caused by an attack which Lord Wolseley, speaking during a discussion raised in the House of Lords by the Duke of Bedford, made upon the existing War Office system, and especially upon Lord Lansdowne, the late Secretary of State. The attack, which was as vehement as it was

MONKEY BRAND CLEANS ALL PLACES!

Cleans Bathrooms.
Cleans Factories.
Cleans Offices.
Cleans Stables.
Cleans Warehouses.
Cleans Workshops.

BROOKE'S SOAP.
MONKEY BRAND.
Cleans Up All Things.
WON'T WASH CLOTHES.

Cleans Armour.
Cleans Equipments.
Cleans Harness.
Cleans Machinery.
Cleans Paints.
Cleans Everything.

Graphic

unexpected, had undoubtedly a certain force; but Lord Lansdowne was justified in pointing out that, if the position of the Commander-in-Chief had been unsatisfactory during the past five years, Lord Wolseley himself was largely to blame. It was a somewhat unedifying discussion, and the country was glad to turn from it to the practical proposals for Army reorganization which Mr. Brodrick made public a few days later. The proposals had for their main object (1) the provision of at least three army corps for foreign service, besides having a properly organized force for home defence; (2) more artillery and mounted troops; (3) reform of medical and transport service; (4) better-trained officers. The Government declined to establish a separate Indian Army, or to adopt compulsion for home defence, being satisfied with the results of a year which " had given us in various forms 140,000 voluntary recruits." The chief practical recommendation was the division of Great Britain and Ireland into six army corps districts—Aldershot, Salisbury Plain, Ireland, Colchester, York, Scotland; the first three army corps were to be entirely Regulars, and the last three were to include sixty battalions and twenty-one batteries of Militia and Volunteers. The Militia were to be raised from 100,000 strength to 150,000 and improved; the Yeomanry were to be raised to 35,000, to be armed with rifles, and to be given extra pay and horse allowance. Special attention was to be paid to the Artillery Volunteers, who were to be " trained for army corps and positions round London." The scheme, though abundantly and deservedly criticized, was accepted as evidence of the new energy imported into the War Office by Mr. Brodrick and Lord Roberts. On May 13, Mr. Brodrick, in the House of Commons, moved a resolution sanctioning his scheme, and this was met by a comprehensive amendment, moved by Sir H. Campbell-Bannerman, which, after a three days' debate, was rejected by 327 votes against 211. The resolution itself was carried by the still larger majority of 305 votes against 163. It is to be feared, however, that no great progress has been really made as yet with the actual organization of the army corps; and, indeed, the first step taken in connexion with the most important of them has had to be undone. Early in the autumn, the command of the First or Aldershot Army Corps, the centre and kernel of the whole Army, was conferred upon Sir Redvers Buller, who had returned to his Aldershot command from South Africa, that of the Second Corps upon the outgoing Adjutant-General, Sir Evelyn Wood, and that of the Third Corps on the Duke of Connaught. At once a voice of protest was raised in the Press; it was pointed out that pledges had been given that only such officers should be appointed to command army corps as would be appointed to command them in actual war, and that, certainly in the first case and probably in the other two, that condition was not fulfilled.

Advertisers in 1901 used political comment to serve commerce: here, Lord Roberts is told how to tackle War Office muddle.

Prudence and Honour

A letter from Edward VII to his nephew, the Czar of Russia, who had written on 4 June to advocate peace by negotiation with the Boers: 19 June.

Suppose that Sweden, after spending years in the accumulation of enormous armaments, had suddenly forbidden you to move a single Regt. in Finland and, on your refusing to obey, had invaded Russia in *three* places, would you have abstained from defending yourself; and, when war had once begun, would you not have felt bound in prudence and honour to continue military operations until the enemy had submitted?

We have every reason to hope that the end is not far off; and we entertain no doubt whatever that, when peace and order have been fully restored, the territories which belong to the two Republics will enjoy in full measure the tranquillity and good government which England has never failed to assure to the populations which have come under her sway.

Graphic

A string of wagons laden with families are taken to camps. During the fighting, farms and farming equipment were destroyed and the country swept bare. The British took care of surrendered burghers' families in camps, while their menfolk continued to fight unhindered by their families.

Below: Emily Hobhouse

WOMEN IN CAMPS

Taking the homeless Boer dependants into camps was intended as a humane move, and even Boer authorities welcomed it at first. But in some bigger camps, ignorance of mass hygiene provisions led to wildfire infection.

The Treatment of Boer Women and Children

The Times, 8 June. Cape Town, 7 June.

Mr. Celliers, a Dutch minister at Aberdeen, writes to the Press praising the humane treatment by the British of the Boer women and children at Port Elizabeth camp. He says that every comfort and convenience is afforded them.

The Concentration Camps

Emily Hobhouse responded to criticism of her report on camp conditions with characteristic vigour and well-marshalled arguments.

The Times, 30 August.

To The Editor.

Sir,—You have honoured me by criticisms of myself and my report in three or four of your columns this morning.

Your correspondent asks three questions:

Firstly: is Miss Hobhouse qualified by any former experience of the country or of war to express an opinion?

It might be asked also, as your correspondent has not been in a concentration camp, is he qualified to criticize the description of one who has? I have no knowledge of war; my work lay amongst some of its results. I went to find out the needs of a homeless people, to help them where possible, and to be able to tell my countrywomen what further relief was necessary. Common sense tells one that the standard of life cannot be the same in wartime as in peace.

Some knowledge of the country and habits of the people is no doubt helpful for a just understanding of how their present hardships press upon them. That knowledge I have been at great pains to acquire by learning from those best fitted to teach, and by visiting such farms and houses as were possible. Moreover, working as I did in close touch with people born and bred in the country I discovered that our views on the camps coincided exactly excepting that mine were the more moderate. These fellow-workers were of various nationalities—English, German, and Dutch.

I fear that the Government Committee just now visiting the camps is subject to the same deficiencies which you ascribe to me. I agree with Mr. Victor Sampson that it is a pity South Africans were not appointed on the committee. Obviously they are best fitted for the work, and I learn that they appealed through their Governor to be represented; it is to be feared without success.

Secondly, your correspondent asks:—Are camps of concentration necessary? To this question he says, I have no qualifications to offer an answer. Certainly I have not, and as I neither ask nor answer the question, one is left wondering why it should be brought into a criticism on my report. All it concerns me to show is that, whether such a policy is or is not a necessary consequence of a war of subjugation, the misery it causes is frightful, and that it is better to encourage and assist than to carp at those who are doing their best to alleviate it.

Thirdly, your correspondent asks:—" Would the women and children be better off in their own homes?" In their own opinion, and in that of all who know and love them best, they would undoubtedly have been better off on their farms. Whether any large number could return now unaided is a different question; but, if not, there is all the more reason for making the camp life healthy and bearable. At any rate they would be better off in the homes of the many friends who apply for their release and apply in vain.

Your correspondent condemns any who " prevent the alleviation of sorrow and affliction in any way " as " unworthy of the name of a man." Is he not himself coming dangerously near that unworthiness? It is easy to disparage. The one great fact of the high mortality he wholly ignores. Of its steady increase he says nothing. Opinion may differ in a thousand ways, but 383 per thousand is a sum total of death too great and awful to explain away. When faced and remembered it scatters to the winds all the comfortable assurances of himself and other writers. The Government return for July gives 1,412 deaths, 1,124 of which were children. This is the death roll for one month out of a total of 93,940 persons. Such a mortality has never been approached by any plague-stricken town in Europe throughout the century. He says I am ignorant, and that is true. But in one piece of knowledge I have an unhappy advantage over him. To my share fell the awful experience of being in the midst of the sickness and suffering which precedes and accompanies such a mortality.

Mr. Victor Sampson argues the people of Kimberley camp are all right because they do not complain. It is true, the Dutch rarely complain; they die. As one writes:—" We will be cheerful and are determined not to let the military think we are cowed or miss our home comforts." The nameless correspondent's sneer about the Boer women whining to me is not only very unworthy of an Englishman but without any foundation in fact.

The sad case of the Johannesburg refugees is again brought forward, it being the common and easy way to disparage work by asking why something else is not done instead. I agree, as your writer says, it is " high time " to give help " more equally " between them and the Boer women. Those refugees, never more than half the number of the Boers now interned in camps and never experiencing a serious mortality, have had a sum of over £240,000 expended on their behalf. Only about 3,500 now remain on relief. In the camps over 90,000 stand in instant need. It is doubtful if the three English funds put together will ever realize £20,000. So far that figure is not approached, and if every obstacle is raised by your writers and others to prevent all knowledge of the truth reaching the English public, there is no likelihood that even so moderate a sum will ever be realized.

It is a continual subject of wonder to me and my friends that those who extol the good management and good condition of the camps should not be desirous of welcoming visits from all who will undergo that labour, instead of jealously excluding all but a few selected ones.

I am, &c., Emily Hobhouse.

Enteric Fever Rages

The Times, 31 August.

Kitchener, preoccupied with the guerillas and their subterfuge tactics and with the civilian farmers aiding them, was singularly ill-equipped and inexperienced when it came to caring for vast herds of women and children.

With regard to these concentration camps there are two main questions which we are entitled to ask of those who criticize the action of our Government and of the military authorities out in South Africa. Will they deny the military necessity of bringing the population together into these camps, or, admitting that necessity, will they assert that the authorities responsible for those camps have shown a deliberate and callous indifference to the sufferings of the refugees put under their charge, and have not done all within their power to make the conditions of their life tolerable and to check the spread of the epidemic which has unfortunately been the cause of so heavy a mortality among the children? To neither of these questions is a clear answer to be found in letters such as the one from Miss Hobhouse which we published yesterday or the one from M. Paul de Villiers which appears in our columns to-day. M. de Villiers asserts that all statements to the effect that the refugees in these camps are well looked after " negatived by the brutal fact that since the establishment of the camps the death-rate for the whole has exceeded 120 per 1,000 per annum," and fortifies his assertions by reference to an article which appeared in one of our contemporaries. He omits the fact, made plain in that article, that the mortality was almost entirely due to an epidemic of measles which broke out among the children in some of the camps, and that in the camps which were not visited by this scourge the death-rate was exceedingly low. Thus, in the Cape Colony camp there were no deaths at all in June out of 390 refugees. But that fact entirely vitiates his whole argument. Heavy mortality for a short period as the result of an epidemic is perfectly compatible with conditions of life otherwise perfectly healthy and satisfactory in every way. We do not wish to deny or minimize the lamentable loss of child life that has taken place in some of the camps. So far from " assuring the British public that the matter was really nothing worth troubling about," we have repeatedly—as, for instance, in the very article to which M. de Villiers takes such exception—expressed our sympathy for the sufferings undergone by Boer women and children as the result of the prolongation of the war. But what we do emphatically deny is that those sufferings have been due to wanton cruelty or deliberate neglect on the

Graphic

General Baden-Powell, later to found the Scouts, enjoyed designing uniforms. To encourage recruitment of nurses, he designed a new kit for them—freely interpreted here by cartoonist H. M. Brock.

part of the British authorities. It is, no doubt, true that, if the Boer refugees had never been brought together in camps, there might never have been so serious an epidemic of measles amongst them. It is equally true that, if Lord Roberts's Army had never been concentrated at Bloemfontein, there would never have been an epidemic of enteric such as raged in that place. In both cases Military necessities brought about conditions which, unfortunately, proved favourable to the spread of disease, and which it took some considerable time to combat.

The necessity of the policy of concentration becomes evident when we consider the character which the war has assumed in the last eight or nine months. The Boer armies have entirely lost coherence, and have been reduced to small bands roving about from farm to farm. For these bands the Boer women on the farms have taken the place of both commissariat and intelligence departments, and have practically been acting as belligerents. Every consideration of expediency would have justified their removal and detention simply and solely as belligerents. But the policy of concentration was mainly due to another consideration, that of humanity. When the guerilla methods of the Boers rendered it necessary to clear the country of supplies, the authorities were presented with the alternative of letting the women and children starve on their farms or of bringing them together and feeding them themselves. The former course might very possibly have been more effective in bringing about the surrender of the Boers. But we decided upon the latter, because we did not wish to have upon our conscience the suffering which the alternative policy might have involved. In this, as in almost everything we have done throughout the war, we have acted with a thought for the future, for the day when we hope to make of the Boers free fellow-citizens in our Empire. M. de Villiers asks us to imagine the feelings of the Boer who returns to his home at the end of the war to find that his children have died in camp. But what would have been his feelings if those children, instead of dying as the result of an epidemic and in spite of the unwearying attendance of British doctors, had perished of starvation deliberately caused by the action of the British troops? Never has there been a war in which one side has derived such advantages from the toleration and humanity of the other. So far from being called upon to " sacrifice their children," as M. de Villiers asserts, the Boers have been enabled by us to dismiss from their minds all considerations of defending or supporting their wives and families, because they know that task is being performed by us in their stead. As Mr. Lawder Eaton pertinently asks, if Miss Hobhouse and those who share her opinions really do believe that what we are doing for these refugees is insufficient, why do they not appeal for help to those, like Mr. Kruger, whose natural duty it is to look after the families of the men whom they encourage to keep up a hopeless and exhausting struggle?

5,000 Dead
Official Facts about the Camp Children

Morning Leader, 19 October.

The statistics issued by the War Office yesterday show that under our care in the Refugee Camps the Boers were dying off during September at the rate of 264 per 1,000 per annum.

The average death-rate in England is 19.

Since 1 June out of 54,326 children 3,209 have died.

Month by month the camps grow worse instead of better.

" The formation of concentration camps has been adopted," wrote Lord Milner a little over a month ago, " purely on military grounds, as a means for hastening the end of the war." They had their beginnings about July, 1900, and as the months went on it became the rule, wherever a column marched, that it should bring back with it every woman or child, and every aged or crippled man whom it found in its path. These people were then regarded as prisoners of war, and shut up in camps surrounded by barbed wire fences, over which sentries watched with loaded rifles. Sometimes women, separated from their children, attempted to escape. They were recaptured, brought back, and punished.

How They Fared

Of the conditions of these camps down to the early months of the present year, we know next to nothing. In January some of them were visited by Miss Emily Hobhouse with the consent of the War Office. A few of them, and these the smaller ones, she found fairly comfortable and well-managed. The larger camps were overcrowded, insanitary, and disease-ridden. Women, accustomed to comfortable and often to wealthy homes, were living huddled together in canvas tents, exposed to the tropical rain, to the bitter cold of the nights, and the burning heat of the days. " Swept up " hurriedly by our columns, they were often in rags and penniless. Their food—and this was our worst failure of duty—was bad and insufficient. A report, dated 9 January, and signed by Dr. Johnston, medical officer of Johannesburg, has been published, condemning samples of the rations supplied as " mouldy," " containing mites," and " unfit for human consumption," and likely to produce disease, " especially in children." Finally a discrimination was made, by which the families of Boers still fighting against us were put on half rations. This has since been altered, and sweeping reforms promised.

From Bad to Worse

Of the real state of these camps there is only one trustworthy index—the death-rate. The full statistics have now been issued for the four months of the South African winter, June to September:

	Total Number in Camps.	Deaths.	Rate per Year per 1,000.
June	85,410	777	109
July	93,940	1,412	180
August	105,347	1,878	214
September	109,418	2,411	264

These figures tell their own tale. It is only necessary to add that they lump together the mortality of men, women, and children, while the good camps help to balance the bad. In Cape Colony during September there were no deaths at all, in Natal only a normal number. It is the big camps outside Pretoria, Johannesburg, and Bloemfontein that are pitched in the valley of the shadow of death.

The Massacre of the Innocents

But the most appalling feature in these figures is the mortality among the children. Among them the annual death rate has risen from 159 per 1,000 in June to 433 in September. Here are the results of the mouldy flour and sugar swarming with mites, the soaking tents and the overcrowding. A race is being exterminated on our hands and under our care. We are told that an epidemic of measles is raging. That was the excuse in June, it is the excuse still. Measles are not commonly a fatal disease

Graphic

THE WAR.

WOUNDED SOLDIERS will derive untold comfort and aid to recovery by the use of CARTER'S APPLIANCES (see below). The benevolent cannot make a more appreciable gift.

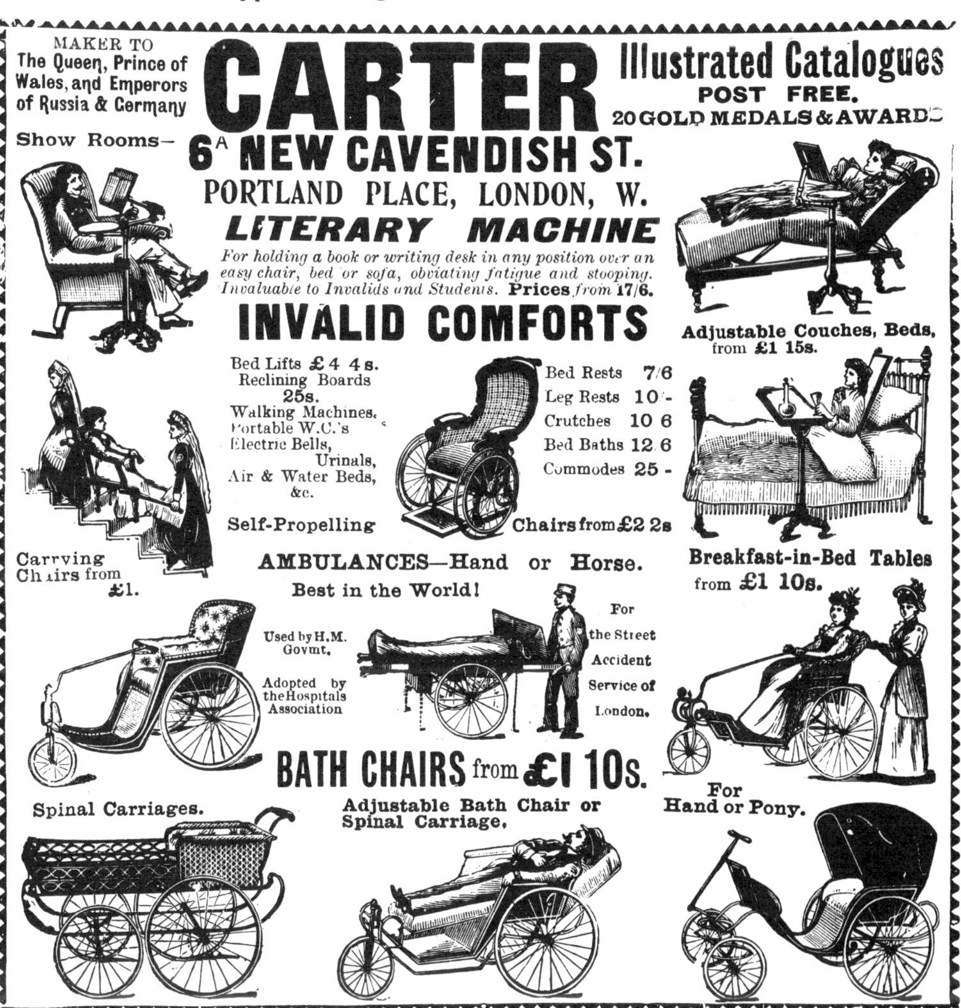

even to children if their diet and general health is otherwise good. But if the camps are full of measles, what has been done to save the healthy children? Nothing: on the contrary, since the close of June 10,000 children have been brought into the camps and subjected to these deadly conditions.

Excuses

We are told that the hardships of the camps mean nothing at all to the Boers. It is said that they lead a dirty semi-civilised, comfortless existence on their own farms. Some have even argued that life in the camps is a luxury to most of these people when compared with the squalor of their homes. If this be true, what does it mean? It means that the Boers are hardy pioneers, apt to endure hardships and make light of privation. And yet such is the state of the camps that the children of these tough backwoodsmen—to use an American term—are dying off in their thousands. How desperately miserable must these camps be if these rough people cannot survive them!

The Remedy

It may be said that these consequences are incidental to war, and therefore that the Boers are as much, or more, to blame than ourselves. But the healthy condition of the camps in the Cape and in Natal is the best answer to that argument. If some camps can be kept free from disease the same conditions ought to avail elsewhere. The real remedy is the remedy proposed long ago by Mr. C. P. Scott, and since advocated by the Cape papers—to remove the unhealthy camps from the Transvaal and the Free State to Cape Colony and the sea coast. There provisions will be less costly, transport will present no difficulty, and it will be possible to send those refugees who have friends to live with their own relatives, while the presence of a civil population will bring public opinion to bear on the camps.

Lord Kitchener, hero of the Sudan war, succeeded Lord Roberts as C-in-C in South Africa. Answering the Boer guerilla tactics, he produced the blockhouse system (opposite).

THE CONSCIENCE OF THE CHURCH

Though the most vociferous critics of the war and the camps were the opposition Liberals, the Church too had voiced the mounting public concern.

The Church and the Camps

Morning Leader, 7 November.

Letter from Mr. Brodrick to the Bishop of Rochester

At the twenty-first session of the Rochester Diocesan Conference, held at the new Chapter House, St. Saviour's, Southwark, yesterday, the President (the Bishop of Rochester) referred to the war.

After commenting on the line which had been taken by a certain section of people in regard to the conduct of the war, and deploring the persistent efforts of some to associate that conduct with cruelty towards the enemy, the Bishop alluded to the

RTHPL

question of the Concentration Camps, and read the following letter he had just received from the Secretary of State for War in answer to inquiries he had made on the subject:

Mr. Brodrick's Reply

" My dear Lord,—You write to ask me whether I can say anything to relieve anxiety as to the mortality in the Concentration Camps in South Africa, and whether the condition of the camps is being ameliorated.

" I can assure you that the subject has received for many months past the most anxious attention on the part of the Government, and of the authorities in South Africa.

" As early as March last, reports were called for on the condition of all the camps, and despite the constant influx of fresh refugees, strenuous efforts were made to secure full supplies of all necessaries and proper sanitation.

" In July a Commission of Ladies was appointed to secure by independent inspection that the camps were all being brought up to the best attainable level, and that where the system of supply was faulty it should be amended.

Fruits of the Commission

" This Commission has been at work throughout August, September, and October, in conjunction with the local authorities. They visited 21 of the camps, and made various recommendations, which Lord Kitchener informs me have all been

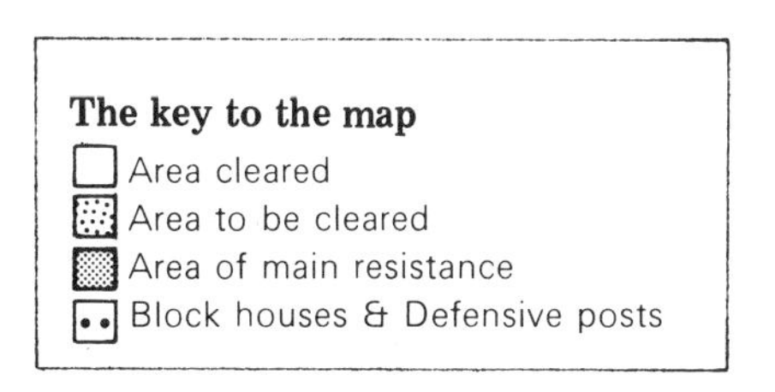

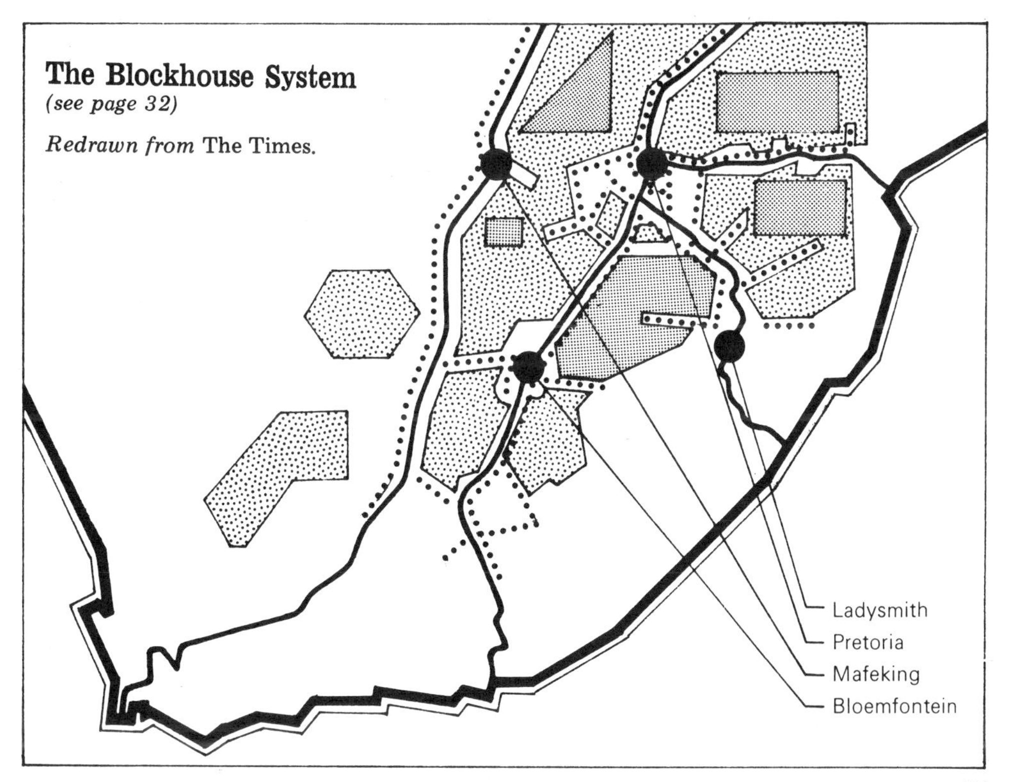

adopted where possible under the circumstances.

" These reports, and the action taken on them, will be made public when received. A large volume of reports from other quarters on these camps is in the Press, and will be distributed in a few days.

" From these it will be gathered that the loss of life in the camps is mainly due to causes incident to a state of war. Families who have undergone severe privations in a country overrun by hostile bands, and who would have starved if they had remained in their homes, were ill-clad and short of food before they came in. They have consequently been unable to combat disease when attacked.

" These conditions have been aggravated by ignorance of ordinary conditions of health, which, with the addition of an epidemic of measles, have made camp life in winter fatal to a large number of children and weakly persons.

Removal to the Coast

" It has been suggested that some of the camps might with advantage be removed to the coast. Such a change would have been most difficult to carry out without suffering during the winter. If, on medical grounds, it is now deemed desirable, which, in view of the difference of climate, is by no means certain, the expense will not stand in the way.

" I need hardly assure you that everything possible to alleviate suffering or prevent mortality is being and will be done, but I hope that those who criticise the results will remember that the losses of our own soldiers, who are in the field, and therefore too often on short rations and without tents, are by no means inconsiderable, and that, with the best will to spare the helpless, no Government can secure the inhabitants of a country from great privation when a small number of desperate men are sparing no means to render it uninhabitable.

I am, yours very truly,
St. John Brodrick."

Help for the Boers

From the diary of a Boer prisoner: 23 September.

Now that our food supply is scarcer, we see more than ever what a service the English have done us in taking away our womenfolk. However severely the defenceless victims of war have had to suffer, they would have had a much worse time of it, and made continuous resistance well-nigh impossible, if the enemy had left them among us. How terribly they would have suffered for want of food and clothing.

ARMY AGAINST GUERILLAS

The Boers resorted to terrorist attacks on such targets as trains and pro-British farms, and to intermittently harassing the Army over too wide an area to be controlled. To contain them, Kitchener crisscrossed the region with barbed wire and fortified posts—the blockhouse system.

The Blockhouse System in South Africa

The Times, 25 December.

The chart [*on page 31*] is intended to illustrate the present military situation in South Africa so far as the distribution of the enemy and the progress made in the blockhouse system are concerned. In order that the situation may be better emphasized, the areas in British and Boer possession have been distinguished by making a variety in shading on the surface of the map. Thus the lighter and dotted shading is intended to mark areas which have been practically cleared of the enemy; in which few supplies, and no large concentrations of Boers are to be found. In such areas it would be possible for small patrols to traverse the country without running across bands of the enemy of greater strength than themselves. The areas which have been totally cleared and in which it is possible for single horsemen to move without immediate fear of molestation are shown on the chart in white. But even in these areas, which for the most part are those which have been enclosed by Lord Kitchener's blockhouses, Boers occasionally will be found who have successfully run the blockade of the defensive posts; but their presence is, of course, a contingency which is becoming rarer every day. The shading with close fine dots depicts the areas to which the Boer resistance is now mainly confined. As will be readily seen, these areas are sections of the theatre of war which are richest in supplies drawn from Kaffirs; are more remote from our railway system, and present the greatest topographical difficulties to the movement of our columns. But, although for the sake of comparison it has been found expedient to show them in heavier shading, it must not be inferred that these areas are of necessity in the undisputed possession of the enemy. They have been crossed and recrossed by our columns, but in spite of this the enemy has invariably returned to them. It is within these areas that the enemy can concentrate in sufficient force to overwhelm any British column that is not at least of the strength of six to seven hundred men. To make a better illustration of the idea embodied in the chart it may be supposed that an officer is attached to a column operating in the Ermelo-Carolina-Amsterdam triangle. He receives a heliogram which informs him that he has been given an appointment in Johannesburg. He determines, for reasons which are immaterial here, to travel as far as possible by road. His column is at Amsterdam. Much as he may desire to push on, he is obliged to remain with his column of 700 men until, moving westward, it strikes the line of blockhouses connecting Ermelo and Standerton. From here, still travelling by road, he is able to push on with the small escort to a convoy which is to ration one of the blockhouse

Morning Leader

KITCHENER: Keep on turning, John. We shall wear him away soon.
JOHN BULL: So they said twelve months ago, and there's no sign of it yet. I am getting rather tired of it.

sections on the Waterval River-Steenkolspruit chain. West of this line the country has been absolutely cleared, and the officer, mounting his pony, is able to ride alone to Springs, where he takes train to his destination.

This clearance of the country and the restriction of the enemy to given and known areas are the direct outcome of Lord Kitchener's blockhouse system. In the chart it has been attempted to show by means of spots the system of ramifications from given centres, in which the blockhouses have been employed in the general scheme of pacification and clearance. By a careful study of all the recent information to hand, it has been possible to arrive at an approximate result which more or less clearly depicts at a glance the remaining energy of the Boers, and the progress of the means which have been adopted for its ultimate subjection. In the first place, the extension of the blockhouse system, so far as it has been officially reported, is substantially correct in the chart. There may be other extensions, in contemplation or in the course of construction, but as they have not yet been reported officially it has been impossible to locate them with any degree of accuracy. But it is fair to conjecture that in the Orange River Colony the Beshof-Kimberley line will connect with Smaldee, that the extension from the east of Kroonstad will, *via* Lindley, ultimately link up with Harrismith, also that in the Transvaal the system of parallels east of the Pretoria—Vereeniging line will be pushed forward until it is impossible for the area north of Ermelo, marked in our chart with fine dots, to exist as a Boer rendezvous.

Limiting the Boers' Mobility

The Times, 4 December

Amid all the harassing work of chasing the Boers from point to point, only to find that at the last moment they vanish into space, it is plain that other work of a more permanently satisfactory kind has been pushed forward. The blockhouse system, by which the movements of all but the smallest groups of the enemy are rendered almost impossible, had been extended two months ago much more widely than most people in this country imagined. We may be sure that it has by this time received considerably greater extension, and that it now opposes a serious obstacle over a great extent of country to the movements of any force important enough to need baggage even upon the limited scale of Boer commissariat arrangements. There are indications that, as the country becomes intersected by these barriers, which cannot indeed prevent evasion but are serious obstacles to concentration, our mobile columns will have a much freer hand in their own districts. Each will have an assigned sphere of operations within which it will have a degree of independence which could not be given so long as each was liable to be suddenly confronted with a Boer force drawn from places far beyond its area. The method is practically that which had to be resorted to for the putting down of the Highland clans. As it is a method of policing a country upon a great scale, it is obviously eminently suited to a war which cannot be ended in any regular manner, but must die out through gradual coercion of rebellious and turbulent elements.

Conventional warfare had to be abandoned for a tactic that would hamper the elusive manoeuvrability of the mounted Boer guerillas. Bit by bit, Kitchener confined them to limited areas, dividing up the country with long barbed-wire barriers which were commanded at intervals by fortified blockhouses from which patrols might maintain the security of the wire.

Redrawn from the Graphic

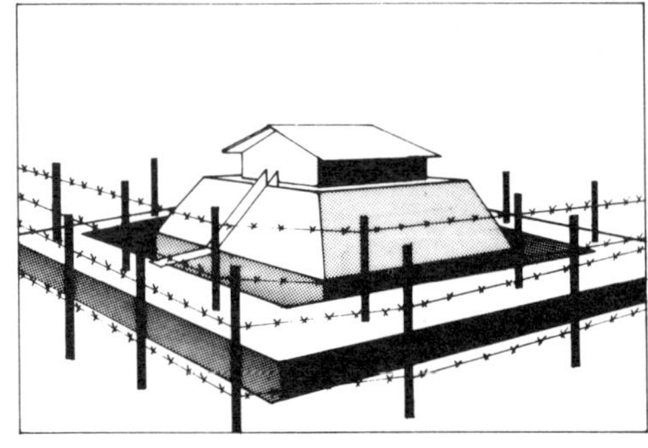

The Wrecking of Trains

Guerilla tactics of the Boers are seen by the British as the outcome of an uncivilized attitude to war.

The Times, 9 September, Pretoria, 7 September.

The outrage of which the Boers were guilty in wrecking a train on the Pietersburg line last Saturday cannot fail to bring home to the minds of every one that we no longer have to deal with an enemy that can claim to be treated in accordance with the rights of civilized warfare.

Though the blockhouse system has materially diminished the risks of railway traffic, it is always possible, with lines of communication extending over several thousand miles, for a few determined Boers to wreck a train. That it is not attempted more often is due to the fact that they prefer to wait until information reaches them as to the possibility of effecting an important *coup.* Such information is conveyed, doubtless, from towns on the railway. The only possible method to stop these treacherous communications, which lead to a sacrifice of the lives of women and children, is to force those likely to give information to the enemy in the field to share the risk of railway travelling. It has therefore very rightly been decided to compel, for the future, the more prominent Dutchmen in towns whose well-known tendencies cause them to be selected for the honour, to accompany passenger trains running through dangerous districts. This salutary measure was adopted in the Franco-German war, and it is hoped that the accurate intelligence of the Boers will prevent these trains from mishap.

The young, Cambridge-educated lawyer, Smuts, led Boer forces against Britain. Later, as Premier of South Africa, he was to be her firm ally.

South African Embassy, London

Chamberlain Provokes the Germans

In Edinburgh, Joseph Chamberlain speaks against foreign criticism.

The Times, 26 October.

" We have not dealt with the rebels or with the guerilla bands with sufficient severity. That is our responsibility; that is the policy of the Government which is questioned. I think that the time has come—is coming—when measures of greater severity may be necessary (Hear, hear and cheers), and if that time comes we can find precedents for anything that we may do in the action of those nations who now criticise our ' barbarity ' and ' cruelty ', but whose example in Poland, in the Caucasus, in the Almeria, in Tongking, in Bosnia, and in the Franco-German war, whose example we have never even approached."

The German View on Camps

The Times, 25 October.

Berliner Tageblatt maintains: " It would be simply an impossibility to intensify the cruelty of the present methods of warfare of the ' butcher ' Kitchener (sic). The allusion to precedents in the war of 1870 for the butcheries (sic) of Kitchener is a piece of impudence against which we must emphatically protest. Mr. Chamberlain was unable to furnish a single precedent for the barbarous herding of defenceless women and children in the shambles of the English concentration camps."

Joseph Chamberlain, a ' Spy ' cartoon.

Vanity Fair

Mansell

Etonian elder statesman of the Liberal party, Rosebery's old-style imperialism estranged many younger Liberals.

Kruger, aged President of the Transvaal, whose intransigence had started the war.

Mansell

LIBERALS AND THE WAR

The Liberal opposition was divided in its attitude to the war. Its Leader, Lord Rosebery, and Herbert Asquith supported it; but David Lloyd-George was gathering adherents for his policy of giving the Boers the independence they were fighting for —including Sir Henry Campbell-Bannerman who was now the Party's Leader in the Commons.

Lord Rosebery on Liberal Policy and the War

The Times, 17 December

This was a momentous speech from the Liberal point of view. Lord Rosebery was sketching in earnest the policy of an alternative Government, and it was not to be the policy foreshadowed by the National Liberal Federation. The war was to be brought to a vigorous close, and we could not be in better hands than Lord Kitchener's, but Lord Rosebery suggested the necessity for a series of special inquiries into possible abuses. Loud were the cheers that greeted the refusal to support foreign falsehoods against our soldiers, but only partial cheering greeted the repudiation of Sir Henry Campbell-Bannerman's allusions to "methods of barbarism." This repudiation was delicately done. The applause was also partial when Lord Rosebery said that he limited his adhesion to the Derby resolutions to the one regarding the concentration camps. Such adhesion was qualified by recognition of the necessities of the case. Breathless interest was shown in Lord Rosebery's sketch of the settlement which he would make. It began with a protest against Lord Milner's Durban speech in so far as it suggested, or seemed to suggest, that no formal settlement could be sought. Without agreeing for one moment to the proposal that we should offer peace, Lord Rosebery insisted on the necessity of being ready to listen to overtures of peace even from the exile Transvaal Government. The recall of Lord Milner or his supersession by a Special Commissioner Lord Rosebery emphatically disapproved, evidently with the approval of the meeting, which loudly cheered his protestations that never in history had been found an instance of a small and defeated nation being held entitled to ask the dismissal of a Minister or Pro-Consul.

Lord Rosebery summarized his settlement policy himself as the grant of the most liberal terms "always excepting the closed and sealed question of incorporation," and wound up his two hours' speech, except for the peroration, which will be memorable in the political history of the country, with the words:—"That represents the best advice I can give the country to-night." Then came a moving scene. He added, with great deliberation, "What I can do to further it, I will do." The vast audience took this promise as they believed it to be meant and made the rafters ring with cheers.

Mr. Asquith at Bilston

Birmingham Daily Post, 20 December.

Mr. Asquith was loudly cheered on rising to address the meeting. He said: "Let me—because it is of importance that we should have this matter clearly in our minds—recapitulate in a very few words what are the main positions put forward by Lord Rosebery, and to which I invite you to subscribe. The first is this, that while keeping our ears open to all reasonable overtures, we should in the meantime pursue our military operations with unflagging vigour and alertness. (Cheers.) That is a condition which is required, not by bloodthirstiness, not by vindictiveness, not by a desire for extermination. It is required by the plainest dictates both of humanity and of prudence. A position which was founded, or which could be plausibly represented as being founded, on our ability to continue and to conclude the struggle would be neither honourable nor lasting. (Applause.) It has taken the best part of a year—and this will be one of the matters which I hope will form a subject of the promised enquiry, why it has taken the best part of the last year—to create a system of mobile columns, with mobile bases, to clear the outskirts of the enclosed and protected area which happily every week grows larger in extent. For the comparative success of this slow and wearisome process—a difficult operation, which I hardly think has any parallel in the military history of the world—the country is prepared to give, and it has given, the acknowledgement of its most hearty gratitude to that great person, General Lord Kitchener.

Boer Independence Gone

The next proposition is this, that it is a fundamental condition of peace that these territories should be permanently incorporated with the Empire as part of the dominions of the King. As Lord Rosebery said the other night, their independence is irrecoverably gone. No one, so far as I know, of any party or section of a party, proposes or dreams that they should be created into Sovereign States. And what is more, no one seriously proposes to repeat the experiment which we tried, and tried in perfect good faith, in the case of the South African Republic, an experiment of a state neither exactly sovereign nor exactly subject; a condition of things which produced, as we now know, the maximum of friction and the minimum either of security or of goodwill. (Hear, hear.) What is the third proposition? The third proposition is that coming under the British flag these territories are to take their place, after as short a period of provisional administration as the exigencies of social and political reconstruction demands, among our self-governing colonies. With this view the conclusion of the war should be followed in Lord Rosebery's words, 'By as just, and prompt, and generous a measure of amnesty as security will allow.' (Cheers.) Now, gentlemen, in both branches of that proposition we are following precedents, and the best precedents in the world. One is almost ashamed, so often has the illustration been used, to repeat it once more, but it will bear studying and restudying and yet studying again. What was it that converted Canada, a country inhabited, as South Africa is, by men of two different races, alien in blood, and in the case of Canada, separated in religion also? What was it that converted Canada from the battleground of warring factions, from the seething hotbed of disloyalty and discontent, to that which it is to-day? It is invidious to make comparisons, but no other colony is more tightly bound by the bond of imperial allegiance and of heartfelt and unaffected loyalty to the Crown and these islands. (Applause.) Canada, which sixty years ago was in open rebellion, a rebellion which had to be put down with much bloodshed, and under conditions of which it is almost impossible to read now without the greatest repugnance. (Hear, hear.) Canada, which sixty or seventy years ago was in open rebellion, has during this war, as we know, furnished regiment after regiment, and is prepared still to furnish contingents so long as contingents are needed. (Applause.)

Local Self-Government for the Boers

The process may be slow; in its earlier stages it may be difficult. But there again you must try as your ultimate aim first of all self-government, and then, as in Canada, federation. (Applause.) As regards the provisional period before the full machinery of the autonomous colony can be set in operation, I have urged myself—and I am obliged to say this, because I see such constant misrepresentations of the views of myself and others who are associated with me—I have urged from the first in the House of Commons, and I cannot say on how many platforms in the country, that from the very earliest moment you should, if you can, associate, even in the provisional administration of the Government, the representatives of both races, both the British and the Dutch. (Hear, hear.) And I see no reason why it should not be tried. Even before you get to the step of the advisory or administrative council, you should introduce the moment the waters of war have subsided, and, thank God, they have now subsided from a large part of the Transvaal—you should introduce in places like Johannesburg and Pretoria, and other comparatively large centres of population, free municipal government. (Applause.) I said a moment ago the process must necessarily be a slow and difficult one. And why? Because you have got to resettle in this unhappily devastated country an expatriated population, and you have, as Lord Rosebery said the other night—and I heartily agree with him—you have to be generous and even, if need be, lavish, in providing the population with means of rebuilding their farms, and restocking their holdings. (Applause.)

THE PRO-BOER DEMONSTRATION.

PLATFORM STORMED: MEETING BROKEN UP.

TOWN HALL WINDOWS SMASHED.

CROWD BATONED BY THE POLICE.

ONE MAN KILLED: POLICE AND ONLOOKERS INJURED.

How Mr. Lloyd George Escaped Disguised as a Policeman

Opposition to the official Liberal policy on the war burst into violence in Birmingham.

Birmingham Daily Mail, 19 December.

Without parallel in the modern history of Birmingham were the scenes enacted both inside and outside the Birmingham Town Hall last night. The famous Afghan meeting which was held during the mayoralty of Mr. Jesse Collings, was a simple affair compared with the pro-Boer demonstration held last night for the purpose of hearing an address from Mr. Lloyd George, the member of Parliament for Carnarvon Boroughs, who attended on the invitation of the Liberal Association. It was not surprising that the visit of this gentleman, who, by his pro-Boer views on the South African War and his personal attacks upon Mr. Chamberlain, has made himself notorious both in and out of Parliament, should evoke a feeling of bitter resentment, which the Liberal party required to recognise, and which culminated in a riot, the outcome of which was that considerable damage was done to the Town Hall, and one young man was killed, and several members of the police force and the general public more or less severely injured. And who, looking at the orderly crowd which was patiently awaiting admission to the hall, could have foreseen the subsequent development of events? The long queue—all ticket-bearing Liberals be it understood, for no one was to be admitted without an authorised piece of cardboard—waited solemnly in the cold frosty air until the doors were opened, and one by one they were admitted. And miserably slow was the examination of tickets, the inspection evidently aiming at the exclusion of anyone not possessing the properly authenticated permit. The very method of passing so large a crowd was certainly not conducive to good order, and this, coupled with the determination to admit only those who favoured Mr. Lloyd George's view, was undoubtedly the primary cause of much of the unpleasantness which subsequently developed. The most elaborate arrangements were made to prevent any unseemly behaviour, but how far these proved a success subsequent events demonstrated.

Vigilant Pressmen

It was perfectly obvious when the meeting broke up in confusion that for Mr. Lloyd George to make his exit in the ordinary manner would be to run the gravest risk of personal injury, and accordingly the police devised an artful dodge whereby he was smuggled out of the hall practically unobserved. This was effected by disguising him as a policeman. The arrangement was intended to be a profound secret, but that did not prevent the affair from reaching the ears of the Pressmen present, who kept a vigilant eye on anybody who left the hall. Passing hurriedly from the platform when the reporters' benches were rushed, Mr. Lloyd George made his way to a private room underneath the orchestra, and there exchanged clothes with a police officer. The pro-Boer champion is, by comparison with the average member of the force, a person of diminutive stature, and as a result some difficulty was experienced in finding an officer whose uniform would fit him. He took it all in excellent part, and laughed amusedly while donning the official dress. Presently he formed up in line with a dozen other officers and marched down the side passage to door L in Ratcliff Place—the door nearest to Paradise Street. He had the helmet drawn well over his forehead, and the chin strap adjusted, and the chances of his being identified were thereby reduced to a minimum. In the crowd, which betrayed quite a savage desire to know the whereabouts of Mr. Lloyd George, the most extraordinary reports were afloat as to his disposal. Some people asserted with a make-believe of authority that he had been hidden in the organ loft, while others were just as positive that he had been secreted in one of the cellars. His actual departure was witnessed by four persons beyond his immediate companions—the Chief Constable, the Deputy Chief Constable (both of whom appeared terribly anxious), and two of the " Mail " reporters. As the line of policemen passed into the street in Indian file, the crowd immediately cleared a passage for them, never for a moment suspecting that the object of their dislike was at that moment in their midst. How dangerous a spirit pervaded the throng was evident from the fierce demeanour exhibited, under a misapprehension, towards the " Mail " reporters, who, on walking through the doorway, were assailed with threatening cries of " Here's some of 'em!" and pushed and hustled in most menacing fashion. The leading lights of local Liberalism who had participated in the meeting remained behind in the committee room, some of them, particularly the ladies, in fear and trembling, at what might ensue if they dared to show themselves outside. In the meantime their friends were seeking an opportune moment to get them away out of harm's reach.

A Convenient Cab

This came with a bugle blast from Victoria Square, which created a rumour that the military had been called out, and by drawing the mob to the front of the Council House, left Radcliff Place by comparison deserted. A cab was standing conveniently opposite one of the doors, and before the few onlookers could realise what had happened Mr. Frank Wright, for whose safety particular apprehension prevailed, had been hustled inside and driven off. His friends dispersed without recognition.

David Lloyd George. Vanity Fair

The Parting of the Ways

Fiery in Parliament and out, backbencher Lloyd George first attracted public attention by his pro-Boer views, which split the Liberal party and provoked Lord Rosebery to emerge from his semi-retirement as the Liberal leader.

Graphic, 29 June.

The most important political question at the present moment is whether the Liberal Party is about to experience another split. The feud between the Liberal Imperialists and the pro-Boers has reached a point where one side or the other must give way. For months past the pro-Boers, led by Mr. Lloyd George, have left no stone unturned to discredit the British Government and blacken the fame of the British Army. The Liberal Imperialists have silently watched this campaign of calumny, abstaining from public protest for fear of destroying the unity of the Party. Their attitude became impossible when Sir Henry Campbell-Bannerman suddenly decided to join hands with the pro-Boers in their atrocity campaign. It was necessary to make an instant protest, and Mr. Asquith made it in language that could not be misunderstood. The question is: What will happen next? The moderate men in both sections are of course trying to salve over the sore, and to insist that the unity of the Party shall at all costs be maintained. It is possible that a superficial unity may be preserved if both sides exercise self-restraint, but real unity is impossible unless one side or the other gives way. At the Queen's Hall meeting the pro-Boers emphatically demanded the restoration of " complete independence " to the two Republics. Sir Henry Campbell-Bannerman has not yet gone so far as this, but he has repeatedly talked vaguely of the duty incumbent upon the Government of bringing the war to an end. The Imperialists, on the other hand, are resolved that the Boer States shall not again have the opportunity of destroying the peace of South Africa, and that the independence they abused shall not be restored. There is no compromise possible between these two policies. What the Boers are fighting for on the veldt is national independence, and Mr. Lloyd-George and Mr. Labouchere are fighting as their allies in the House of Commons. Until Boers and pro-Boers alike are prepared to accept defeat, the war must go on—the war of bullets in South Africa and slanders at Westminster. It is impossible, under such conditions, for the nominal Leader of the Opposition to resume his favourite seat on the fence. He must either frankly dissociate himself from the pro-Boer demand for Boer independence, or he must be content to see the Liberal Party shattered.

Little Englanders

" Little Englanders " was the label given to pro-Boers, with which Liberal Sir Henry Campbell-Bannerman was now identified.

The Times, 31 December.

Sir Henry Campbell-Bannerman so studiously endeavoured to please both sections of the Opposition that he distinctly lost ground with both until the autumn, when the increasingly pro-Boer character of his speeches seemed to mark him definitely as belonging to the anti-Imperialist section. An absolute break-up of the party has indeed been avoided, but the essential differences remain as acute as ever. At the beginning of June advantage was taken of the presence in London of Messrs. Merriman and Sauer, the delegates of the Afrikander Bond, to organize a pro-Boer meeting in the Queen's-hall, with Mr. Labouchere in the chair. The meeting was stormy, but great efforts were made, both at home and abroad, to represent its resolutions as conveying the views of the mass of Liberals throughout the country. A special feature of this meeting, and of pro-Boer speeches and writings generally, was venomously to attack the High Commissioner, who came to England in the early summer—nominally for a period of rest. He had a great reception, and was made a peer on his arrival; and it need hardly be said that his " rest " was a time of hard work, almost from the beginning to the end. Early in July Mr. Asquith found it necessary, at a dinner in the City, to protest in the most formal way against the identification of the Liberal party with the policy of the Little Englanders and the pro-Boers. A meeting was called at the Reform Club on July 9, and a vote was passed expressing confidence in Sir Henry Campbell-Bannerman, both wings agreeing for the moment to permit what they were pleased to call " honest differences of opinion " on the question of the day. The futility of this eirenicon was unexpectedly brought home to the world, a week later, by a letter from Lord Rosebery to the City Liberal Club, in which, with unkind frankness, he expanded this phrase into " an honest and irreconcilable division of opinion on a group of questions of the first importance." He added that " one school or the other must prevail if the Liberal party is once more to become a force "; and that till that time arrived to talk of the grand old principles of Liberalism was all very well for a peroration, but was not

Jingoist politics were used in 1901 to sell anything from soap to tobacco.

Graphic

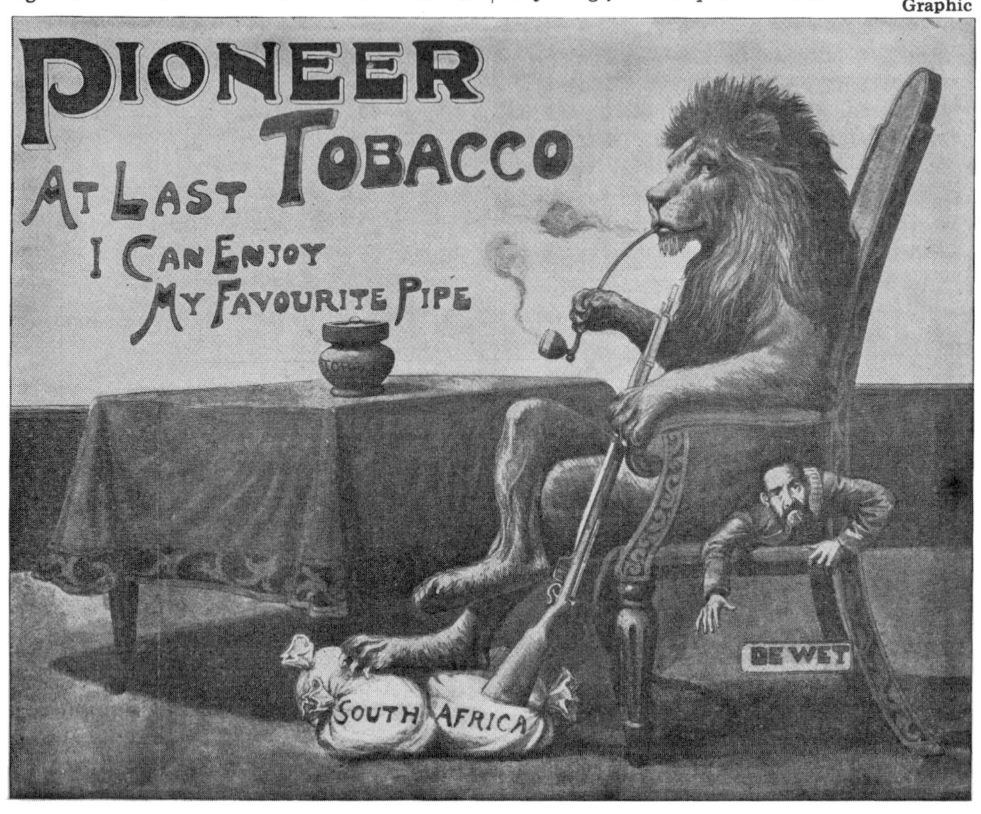

business. The depth of the cleavage became more and more evident, as time went on and Sir Henry Campbell-Bannerman kept repeating his deplorable language about " methods of barbarism "; and it became more and more apparent that, unless some *deus ex machina* intervened, the party must break up. Hence the extraordinary interest aroused by the announcement that Lord Rosebery would speak at Chesterfield on December 17: an event which was held to be equivalent to, or at least to foreshadow, his resumption of the leadership of the party. His speech did, in fact, lay down a policy, and gave a real opportunity to the Opposition to reorganize itself; but it remains to be seen whether the speaker has any intention of following it up in the only effective way—by definitely accepting the responsibility, and the drudgery, that falls to the head of a party.

AT THE YEAR'S END

Though the British were getting weary of the inconclusive war, victory and restoration of order and progress were never doubted.

South Africa

Saturday Review, 28 December.

To the uninitiated newspaper-reader the fighting in South Africa must often have resembled nothing so much as a game of blindman's buff, in which the Boers dealt swift blows against a clumsy enemy, whose grip, however, they could not always elude. But now, as we look back upon the year's operations, we can discern both the method and result of Lord Kitchener's plan. It was (1) to keep the Boers moving, and so prevent them from concentrating any force sufficient for a serious attack; (2) to protect the railways by blockhouses and so set free as many men as possible for the pursuit of the commandos; (3) to rope off the chief industrial areas in the Transvaal, Orange River, and Cape Colonies, so that the resumption of normal life within these districts need not be delayed until the last commando was destroyed; and (4) to push the lines of these protected areas outwards, and gradually drive the Boer guerillas back into the wastes, where they would be comparatively harmless. At the same time a greater or less proportion of the forces at Lord Kitchener's disposal have been continuously engaged in reducing the number of the Boers in the field.

Normal Life Returns

Thus Lord Kitchener had not only to reduce the Boers, but also to prepare the way for the resumption of industrial life at the first possible opportunity. When the third stage was reached, Lord Milner returned from England, and took up the task of constructing a scheme of civil administration. If we may judge from the tone of the political speeches recently delivered, the items of his progress, doled out in telegraphic messages, have produced little effect upon the public mind. But these items, when summarised, show a significant advance.

The main lines of railway, which converge on Johannesburg from Capetown, Port Elizabeth, Durban, and Delagoa Bay, are provided with rolling stock and ready for traffic. Even Rhodesia can get its mining plant through from Capetown. With food supplies assured, the Outlanders are being allowed to return in increasing numbers. On the Rand more mines are being worked every week, the Stock Exchange has been opened, provision has been made for an adequate supply of native labour, and the streets of Johannesburg have resumed their normal appearance. In the protected area of the Orange River Colony the grip of military exigencies is also relaxed. The railway brings supplies to Bloemfontein in sufficient quantities to make it unnecessary for the military authorities to supervise and distribute them. Prices are once more fixed, not by proclamation, but by supply and demand. And here too the mines are resuming work. In the Transvaal the administrative problems which are directly connected with the gold industry have been taken in hand. A code of laws regulating the relations between the native labourers and their European employers has been proclaimed. By the provisions of this code the native is protected against oppression and robbery at the hands of unscrupulous agents; and the liquor traffic—the chief cause of the insubordination and incapacity of the native employee—has been sternly repressed. Under the new administration to supply a native with liquor becomes an offence punishable by severe penalties. The necessity of the " pass " system in the interests of public security is recognised; but, while the system is maintained, modifications have been introduced which will protect the educated native from unnecessary humiliation, and the coloured population in general from petty oppression. A commission, over which Sir Richard Soloman, the Transvaal Attorney-General, presides, is considering the existing gold laws, with a view to introduce such modifications as the best local experience and the financial interests of the colony may suggest: and thus the way is being prepared for that extension of the gold industry which is expected to be one of the first results of the establishment of British rule. Even as it is, the awakening industrial life of the Rand has provided the civil administration of the colony with a revenue sufficient for its present needs.

Farming and Irrigation

These are measures which promise the restoration and expansion of the industrial life of South Africa at no distant date. Even more significant are two small items of information, which, unsensational as they are, nevertheless embody the commencement of an all-important enterprise. Some months ago it was reported that Mr. Willcocks, of the Egyptian Irrigation Service, was in Pretoria, devising a scheme of irrigation for the Transvaal and Orange River Colonies. More recently we learnt that the first Yeomen settlers had been established on Government farms in the latter colony, and that the Land Settlement Board had sown some 8,000 boxes of French seed potatoes. Readers of the *Saturday Review* will not need to be reminded of the importance of irrigation and English immigration—irrigation to fertilise the barren veldt, English immigrants to settle on the land and mingle with the Boers. In these two measures we have the key to the nationality difficulty in South Africa. Progress in the direction of these measures is progress of the most vital kind.

The Camps

This record is the more creditable in view of the fact that in the midst of his legitimate administrative work Lord Milner was called upon to reform the Concentration Camps. The decision to break up the larger camps into camps of more manageable size, and to place the whole system under the supervision and control of officers experienced in the management of the plague and famine camps in India, is a wise one. It promises to close an ugly matter. But of all the hopeful signs of the last three months the presence of Mr. Willcocks and the settlement of these British Yeomen convey the most assured prospect of ultimate success. They mean that England has done well to place its confidence in Lord Kitchener and Lord Milner: that the time will come when South Africa will be no longer " the grave of reputations ", but a record of the courage and endurance of the British army and an example of what a nation's resolution can effect.

PRESS DISTORTIONS

In the days before army press officers, the responsibility for decisions on what was to be told and what was not fell within the competence of the commander in the field. He was often too busy to deal effectively with a press and public hungry for news.

The " Land of Lies "

Morning Leader, 11 June.

Mr. Brodrick betrayed no sense of the gravity of the question he was handling in his reply to Mr. Dillon last night. It is so far satisfactory to learn that the correspondents who have been guilty of telegraphing flagrantly false news will be "dealt with." Certainly, if journalists at the front are to be subjected to a quasi-military discipline, the authors of these inventions ought not to go unnoticed. Moreover, if the privilege of sending news is to be jealously restricted, it ought to be reserved for men more worthy to use it. We learn little enough from official sources. Our unofficial chroniclers invent for us victories that have no foundation in fact, while they blacken with an impartial pen the character of the combatants on either side. We need not repeat again what we wrote yesterday about the defeat of Beyers' commando, which never occurred. Reuter's agency will doubtless take steps to safeguard its reputation in future. But while we censure Reuter's correspondent for his sensational telegram, elaborating with imaginative detail some untested breath of camp gossip, what are we to say about the reticence of Lord Kitchener, who has not yet mentioned in his dispatches an engagement near Pienaars River on 1 June, in which we lost seven killed and eighteen wounded?

Publication of Correspondence

The manufacture of news is only one aspect of the question. Hardly less serious is the suppression of news. Lord Kitchener is a busy man, but it is high time that a competent officer was attached to his staff whose duty it should be to record events as they occur day by day in an adequate summary. Another simple reform would be the liberation of correspondents' letters from the censorship. A letter which is a month old when it is published in London cannot possibly give away any valuable information to the enemy. There is, further, the question which Mr. Dillion broached—the exclusion from the two Republics of the correspondents of all but the Ministerial journals. So long as that arrangement continues the public may make up its mind that it will learn through the Press only so much of the truth as serves the interests of the party in power. Mr. Brodrick's answer that Lord Kitchener is in "complete ignorance of the politics of all the papers" is merely imbecile. Lord Kitchener is not the censor, nor yet is he an ignoramus.

HOME THOUGHTS ON WORDS FROM ABROAD

Attacks in foreign press reports on British conduct of the war hurt the amour propre *of politicians and others. It was felt to be necessary to answer the criticisms from the more impressive sources.*

Foreign Criticism

The Times, 9 August.

The Radicals and the whole herd of our foreign critics, including the nation responsible for the hideous massacres of last summer in Manchuria, profess the deepest concern at our methods of warfare. The Belgian Socialists are so profoundly moved that they are going to propose a Socialist congress upon our sins. Perhaps the sufferings of the natives in the Congo Free State might occupy them to more advantage. The truth, of course, is that never in the history of war has such leniency been shown to an enemy as we have consistently shown to the Boers. Has any Continental nation ever yet accorded to small roving bands of men in civil dress the full privilege of belligerents? Would any Continental nation dream of doing so to-day? We know Bismarck's views on the subject from Dr. Busch. He denounced the "treacherous franctireurs who now stand in their blouses with their hands in their pockets, and in the next moment when our soldiers have passed by take their rifles out of the ditch and fire at them." "It will come to this," he added, "that we will shoot down every male inhabitant." That was a savage threat which we should be glad to think that even Bismarck would never have wished to execute. But it illustrates very clearly the way in which many foreigners, who now join in and relish the Radical cant about our "methods of barbarism," would punish the acts of treachery we daily condone.

Race-Hatred

Unrestrained crowing is found distasteful in Britain.

Morning Leader, 17 September.

We have received a copy of a weekly paper called the *Owl* published in Cape Town. This paper, it must be remembered, circulates freely in South Africa, while the Dutch papers are confined to Cape Town and its environs. In it, we find the following diatribe by a regular lady contributor of the *Owl's*, the person who claims to speak for " Society " in its pages:

You would never believe how this sort of life—this knuckling down in trifles under the thumb of the hitherto despised Englishman—has taken the starch out of the Dutch people. Martial Law is the grandest inspiration that ever entered the military grade.... Far more demoralising in its effects than lyddite fumes (for these but destroy the body whilst the other is felt in the soul), by the commandeering of horses and cattle, and the regulations concerning passes, martial law has driven home to the Dutch in a way no other method could possibly have accomplished, the fact that Britain means to settle once for all the question of superiority in the Colony.... The loss of their horses and carts . . . the fact that not more than four may talk together at a time . . . that their ministers are spoken to like children, and liable at any moment to be deported; the inability to move anywhere without a pass—all this has impressed the rebel Dutch with a sense of England's power, as no brilliant series of victories could have done. Verily the iron of it has entered into their souls. I stood outside the Dutch Church and listened to their singing. The old defiant ring and sonorous gladness were no longer there, and every now and then a strong man's voice trembled. Through it, and underneath it all, there breathed the cry of the spirit: " How long, O Lord! How long!"

This, be it remembered, is a eulogy of martial law. How many of us had realised before what race-hatred means?

Graphic

Protesting Irish MPs were lifted bodily out of the House of Commons by policemen.

The police had no easy task. For instance, in order to remove Mr. Cullinan, they had to pass along benches occupied by Irish members. After a long struggle the honourable member was dragged over two benches on to the floor of the House and carried out amid loud Irish cheers. Police and Nationalists were by this time one confused, struggling mass. Mr. Flavin gave much trouble. He sank as low as he could in his seat, reduced himself as nearly as possible to the condition of a log, and had to be bodily carried out.

Irish and the Closure

Despite progressive land reforms, the Fenian (Catholic/Republican) movement gained in strength. Lacking any Parliament of their own, Irish MPs used Westminster as a platform for their demonstrations; and the theatres in Ireland staged plays with fiercely revolutionary themes.

Disgraceful Scenes

Daily Chronicle, 3 January.

Soon after midnight the most discreditable and disorderly scene ever witnessed in Parliament occurred. The matter at issue was that the Irish Members objected to the Vote on account being closured because they had had no opportunity of discussing Irish affairs upon it, and they refused to leave the House when the question was put and go into the division lobbies. The recalcitrants numbered about sixteen, no very prominent members of the party, such, for instance, as Mr. Dillon or Mr. J. Redmond, being included among them. As they refused to leave the House the Chairman of Committees summoned the Speaker, who resumed the chair and called upon them to " clear the House," as the Chairman had directed them to do. This demand was met by disorderly cries and emphatic refusals.

Police Summoned to the Commons

The Irish Members concerned sat in a solid mass on the benches below the gangway, and flatly refused to obey the Speaker's order to leave the House—their number was uncertain, but seemed to range between sixteen and twenty. Mr. Balfour moved that these gentlemen be suspended from the service of the House, and a division upon it was challenged, and the motion declared carried. The Speaker then asked the Members in question to leave the House, but Mr. Flavin, who had been named, flatly declined. The Serjeant-at-Arms was called upon to execute the orders of the House, and the efforts of the doorkeepers who were called in proving unsuccessful, the police were summoned, and an unprecedented scene followed. In the historic event of a good many years since Members did withdraw, if under protest, when actually directed to do so by the officers of the House, now they flatly refused, amid shrill defiant cries. The police were summoned—at one time there were some fifty officers on the floor of the House, and Mr. Crean, struggling violently, was literally carried out of the Chamber. Members generally stood aghast. The Ministerial benches were crowded, most of their occupants standing to witness this extraordinary episode in the history of the House. We need not prolong the painful story. While the lamentable scene was in progress other Members of the Nationalist party were howling and struggling, some singing the while " God Save Ireland," " The Wearin' of the Green," and other patriotic songs. The scene ended between one and two o'clock.

ENDS OF THE EARTH

The uninhabitable five million square miles of the Antarctic, with ice up to 2,000 feet thick, had attracted few explorers—and none had tried to reach the Pole, until Scott's first expedition.

The Antarctic Expedition

Graphic, 30 March.

The " Discovery," which has been specially built for a new British Antarctic expedition, was launched last week from the yard of the Dundee Shipbuilders' Company. The vessel, which, when completed, will cost about £50,000, has occupied fully a year in building, and is considered the strongest and most efficient exploring ship which has ever left these shores. Although little hope is entertained that the " Discovery " will reach the South Pole, Captain Scott and the little company of adventurers who go with her mean to penetrate further into the Southern Polar regions than anyone has gone before, and the deep interest attaching to exploration within the Antarctic Circle has been fully demonstrated by Mr. Borchgrevink's narrative, recently published, of his experiences in the " Southern Cross." The desirability of Antarctic exploration has long been recognised, but at the same time it has been felt that the undertaking was so great, so difficult, and so dangerous that it could only be attempted by Government and by the Navy.

In One Season

The Government, for various reasons, has not felt able to undertake the work and ensure its end. Great credit is therefore due to the Royal Society and the Royal Geographical Society for the part which they have taken in making possible and organising the present expedition. Sir Clement Markham has expressed as his opinion that there is very little doubt that there is no part of the great ice mass in the Antarctic regions which might not be penetrated by a good ship and a resolute and intelligent captain, and it is hoped that in one navigable season the " Discovery " will be able to penetrate far enough to the eastward of the extreme east reached by Ross, to gather many new facts about the ice barrier, which is one of the most extraordinary phenomena on the earth.

If " Discovery " succeeds in doing so much, it is proposed that in a second season she shall go further still to the eastward, or, if the commander judges it better, start from Ross's most westerly point. There will thus be one winter and one spring, possibly two winters and two springs, to be devoted to a series of observations and making discoveries by land. The Antarctic Circle, according to our present knowledge, can only be attacked from one point—namely, Victoria Land, first discovered by Sir James Ross—and to Victoria Land the " Discovery " will go as direct as may be possible. How far eastward she may then be able to penetrate depends on the obstacles offered by the great ice mass, which, drifting south every year, forms such a formidable barrier.

Funds Still Required

How keenly interest has been awakened on the subject of Antarctic exploration is shown by the fact that there are now being organised German, Swedish, and Scottish Antarctic expeditions. The German expedition has been largely successful in obtaining funds from the German Government through the whole-hearted support of the German Emperor, and so suffers from no lack of support, as is the case, in spite of private munificence, with the others, but the Scottish expedition is nevertheless expected to start in the coming autumn. With regard to the voyage of the " Discovery," though a large amount has been subscribed, £30,000 is still required, which sum, it is hoped may soon be raised.

Launched in Scotland and victualled on the River Thames, Scott's ship for the first journey to the Antarctic, the Discovery, *is now permanently moored on the Thames.*

Graphic

North and South Polar Expeditions

Captain Scott prepares for his great adventure. Graphic, 15 June.

Rapid progress has been made with the fitting out of the *Discovery*, which was launched at Dundee some weeks ago, and the vessel has arrived in the Thames, where she is to take in her stores and equipment previous to her departure for the Antarctic. Sir Clement and Lady Markham, and Captain Scott, who will command the expedition, are on board. When the work of fitting the vessel has been completed a visit of inspection will be paid by the committee who have promoted the undertaking. After that it is intended to throw the ship open to the public. While at Dundee the *Discovery* was berthed in Victoria Dock, and it is a rather remarkable circumstance that, for a little while, there lay alongside of her the *America*, shortly to sail for the North Pole.

When We Come Home

A letter from Captain Scott, written early in the voyage.

My own dearest Mother,
It is so nice to get your brave letter, but indeed I don't think there is the least cause for anxiety. All you have to do is to take the greatest care of yourself and be ready for all sorts of good times when we come home.

The ship is a magnificent sea boat, smooth and easy in every movement, a positive cradle on the deep. We only sigh for more sails. Ours are made for tempestuous seas, so they look rather like pocket handkerchiefs in a light Trade; they are so small that even in a hurricane they couldn't capsize the ship. I'm a little disappointed with her speed. We want very favourable conditions to keep up 7 knots.

The fellows in the wardroom are beginning to get on splendidly and we have very cheerful times at meals. Of course it is all yachting and comfort so far. The trying conditions are not yet arrived.

I like Wilson more and more. *Entre nous* his, Skelton's and Barne's are the three characters that attract me more than any other on board. Wilson is a little more serious than the others.

Scamp [*his dog*] is distinguishing himself on all sides. He was landed for the first time yesterday and his enjoyment was the delight of all beholders.

My dearest, I do hope you will have a nice quiet holiday. You certainly have earned it, for I fear my affairs gave you a good deal too much to do before we left.

Best of love, dear.

Your affect. son

A Great Adventure Begins

Scott's diary.

"The wind had died away; what little remained was reflected in a ghostly glimmer from the white surface of the pack; now and again a white snow petrel flitted through the gloom. The grinding of the floes against the ship's side was mingled with the more subdued hush of their rise and fall on the long swell, and for the first time we felt something of the solemnity of these great southern solitudes."

Captain R. F. Scott, RN, leader of the expedition to the Antarctic, at his desk during the preparations. **Graphic**

An Alliance Vaulted

Technical and industrial progress had given Germany a new self-confidence; and she felt she could demand Britain's total commitment to an alliance—Britain was isolated, and both France and Russia were hostile to her. But the Kaiser's activities made Britain wary; devoted though he had been to his grandmother Victoria (though not to her son Edward VII) he was, in a fervour of nationalism, building up his navy to a menacing size.

Approaches to Britain, and Cabinet reactions to them, were kept secret from Parliament and Press. They were made at a country house-party, to Edward when he attended the funeral of the Kaiser's mother (Edward's sister), at private meetings, and via a Times *representative in Germany. While Lansdowne (Foreign Secretary) at first was inclined to listen, and had no aversion to secret alliances, Salisbury (Prime Minister) stood firmly by his belief in " splendid isolation "; and his masterly memorandum of 29 May was a decisive influence on the Cabinet.*

When Chamberlain's anti-German speeches made the British Government's attitude public, negotiations finally petered out completely.

To Stand Alone

Cabinet memorandum by Salisbury, 29 May.

Neither we nor the Germans are competent to make the suggested promises. The British Government cannot undertake to declare war, for any purpose, unless it is a purpose of which the electors of this country would approve. If the Government promised to declare war for an object which did not commend itself to public opinion, the promise would be repudiated, and the Government would be turned out. I do not see how, in common honesty, we could invite nations to rely upon our aids in a struggle, which must be formidable and probably supreme, when we have no means whatever of knowing what may be the humour of our people in circumstances which cannot be foreseen.

RTHPL

Kaiser William II was a disastrous dabbler in international politics.

After the Boxer Rising

The Boxers were a secret society in China (so-called because boxing was a part of their ritual), dedicated to ousting the foreign powers who, through warfare, had secured unfair trading rights in China and whose missionaries threatened ancient religious beliefs. The Boxers rose in 1898, and in 1899 received the support of the imperial government of China under the Dowager-Empress. Massacres of foreigners and a siege of embassies followed, which provoked military intervention, the routing of the Boxers, and the flight of the Dowager-Empress.

In 1901 a settlement was negotiated (the Boxer Protocol) whereby the foreign powers were to be paid a large indemnity, but there was no carve-up of her territories among the victors: Britain, Russia, France, Germany, Japan, U.S.A. Germany was particularly intent upon exacting not only huge indemnities but the maximum humiliation of Chinese leaders.

Prince Tuan and the Silken-Girdle Death

Glasgow Evening News, 9 January.

Glasgow Evening News

In the Joint Note presented by the Powers to China there is a clause which demands

Below: A British officer poses in a mandarin's costume given to him by friendly villagers.

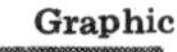

Graphic

" the most severe punishment " of the high officials who were concerned in the Boxer rising. The most notorious of these is Prince Tuan. Li Hung Chang asserted that he could not be put to death, being an Imperial Prince. But this plea is not supported by precedent, as is made evident by a few facts about

his family history.

Tuan is the descendant of a half-brother of a Chinese Emperor, and was only a beila, or ordinary member of the Imperial clan, till 1894, when the Emperor raised him to the grade of a Prince of the Second Rank.

If then, says a writer in the *Daily Chronicle*, the elder brother could be

punished by death.

Prince Tuan can also receive a similar sentence. If he escapes his deserts, he will surely wreak vengeance sooner or later on his denunciators, and his escape will be accepted by the Chinese as a proof of the weakness and vacillation of the European Powers.

He is the third son of Prince Tuan. His elder brother, Tsai-Yuen, Prince of I, was a prominent leader of the extreme anti-foreign party in 1859-60, just as much as Prince Tuan is to-day. It was he who imprisoned Europeans, who broke faith at Tungchow, and who declared war when peace had been practically concluded.

But he was not punished for his anti-foreign policy.

He escaped scot-free

for the cruelties inflicted on his unfortunate prisoners. In the year 1861, on the death of the Emperor Hien Fung, he was left in charge of the government as President of a Council of Regency.

This did not suit the present Empress-Dowager and her allied Empress Tsi An, the legal widow of Hien Fung.

They arrested Tsai-Yuen, the Prince of I, sentenced him to death, and sent him the silken girdle wherewith he might commit the happy dispatch in accordance with the privileges of the Imperial House.

The Chinese Peace Negotiations

Graphic, 19 January.

After infinite discussion the " irrevocable " demands of the Powers in China have been duly signed on behalf of the Empress, first by Prince Ching, and subsequently by Li Hung Chang. There is little doubt that some part of the delay in accepting the conditions was caused by the fact that the Chinese were well aware that some of the Powers thought the terms excessively hard and the Court more than hoped that procrastination might bring about some modification of the

Prince Ching did much to restore peace in China by negotiating terms with the foreign powers.

Graphic

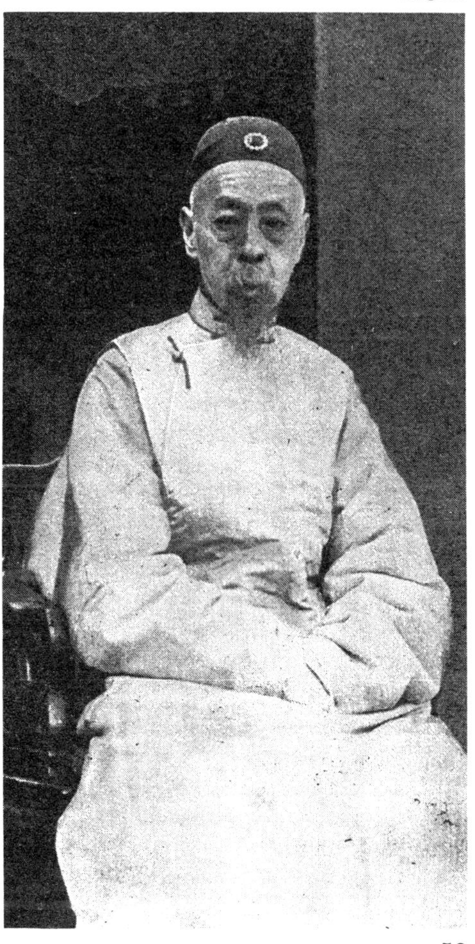

demands. However, last Friday the two Chinese Plenipotentiaries received permission to sign the Protocol, the directions coming in the shape of a telegraphic edict which also authorised the use of the Imperial seal on the documents signed. Prince Ching thereupon asked permission of the Japanese Commandant to enter the Forbidden City to get the seal, leave being at once granted. At an earlier stage of the proceedings the Empress telegraphed to the plenipotentiaries forbidding them to sign, but subsequently reconsidered her attitude. Among those who advised her not to give way was the Viceroy Chang Chi-hung, but this official, after reading the telegrams from Prince Ching and Li Hung Chang to the Empress giving her contrary advice, with excellent reasons therefore, altered his mind, realising that he had made a mistake and had committed the serious crime of giving the Throne bad advice. The twelve articles of the Joint Note which had to be accepted before the Allies could hold out any hope of evacuating Peking and the province of Chi-Li are couched in the following terms:

The first requires an Imperial Prince to go to Berlin to express the regret of the Emperor of China and of the Chinese Government at the assassination of Baron von Ketteler, and the erection of a commemorative monument on the scene of the assassination, with inscriptions expressing the regrets of the Emperor.

The second article demands the severest punishment of the persons designated in the Imperial Decree of September 25, and of those whom the representatives of the Powers may designate. The article also requires the suspension, for five years, of official examinations in those cities where foreigners were massacred or cruelly treated.

The third article demands that honourable reparation be made to Japan for the murder of M. Sugiyama, the Chancellor of the Japanese Legation.

The fourth article stipulates that an expiatory monument shall be erected in every foreign and international cemetery which has been desecrated or in which graves have been destroyed.

In the fifth article the maintenance is demanded, under conditions which the Powers shall determine, of the prohibition of the importation of arms and of materials exclusively used for the manufacture of arms and ammunition.

The sixth article requires the payment of equitable indemnities for the Governments, societies, companies, and individuals, and for the Chinese who have suffered in consequence of being employed by foreigners in China, and stipulates that China shall adapt measures acceptable to the Powers for guaranteeing the payment of such indemnities.

In the seventh article the right of each Power is laid down to maintain a permanent Legation guard and to put the Diplomatic quarter in a defensible condition, with the stipulation that the Chinese shall not be allowed to reside in that quarter.

The eighth article provides for the destruction of all the forts which might obstruct free communication between Peking and the sea.

The ninth article asserts the right of the Powers to occupy certain points with military forces to maintain communication between Peking and the sea.

The tenth article requires the publication for two years in all sub-prefectures of an Imperial decree embodying a perpetual prohibition of membership of any anti-foreign society under penalty of death, enumerating the punishments inflicted on the guilty, and the suspensions of examination in the cities referred to above. The issue of an Imperial decree is also demanded, ordering that all officials responsible for the maintenance of order in their jurisdiction shall be removed permanently and disqualified from office and honours in the event of a renewal of the anti-foreign disturbances or other infractions of the Treaty, which are not immediately suppressed with the punishment of the guilty.

The eleventh article lays down that China shall negotiate amendments to the treaties of commerce and navigation which the Powers regard as useful and proper, and shall also negotiate upon other matters pertaining to commercial relations with the object of facilitating them.

The twelfth article provides that China shall determine in what manner to reform the department of foreign affairs, and shall modify Court ceremonials regarding the reception of foreign representatives in the manner indicated by the Powers.

The Indemnity Question

Each of the powers staked a claim for heavy financial reparations to be paid by China. Excessive demands, by Germany and Russia particularly, threatened to ruin China.

The Times, 27 May

Shanghai, 10 May, via *Rangoon, 26 May.* The scale upon which several of the Powers have formulated their claims has created a feeling akin to consternation as indicating a determination to deny China all reasonable chance of recuperation. At the same time, it illustrates once more the hollowness of the so-called Concert of the Powers, for a nominal agreement upon the principle of the indemnity cannot disguise a profound divergence of methods in its application. Even after every allowance is made for the greater distance which the Continental contingents had to be conveyed and for the relative cost of the maintenance of European and Asiatic troops, the difference between the British claims on the one hand and those of Germany, Russia, and France on the other cannot be accounted for except by a fundamental difference of aims. How, for instance, can the claims for military and naval expenditure, if honestly framed on identical principles, amount in the case of Great Britain to less than £5,000,000, while those of Germany amount to £15,000,000, France £11,000,000, and Russia £17,500,000, allowing even that the last-named includes also compensation for the damage done to the Siberian railways, whereof the extent appears to have been grossly exaggerated? Even Japan, despite the exigencies of the financial situation at home, only claims £3,500,000. Yet Japan contributed the largest and most efficient fighting force at the beginning of the operations, and Great Britain has maintained actually the largest fighting force throughout the whole period.

Crushing Burden

The insistency displayed in certain quarters upon immediate payment of the indemnity in some form readily convertible into cash emphasizes this indifference to the future interests of China. It is intelligible enough that nations which, like Russia and France, have hardly any material interests in China and can therefore disregard the inevitable consequences of imposing a crushing burden upon the Chinese people, should insist upon their pound of flesh, but that Germany with her growing commercial aspirations should adopt the same attitude can only tend to revive the suspicions to which her Far Eastern policy has so frequently given rise.

These apprehensions are naturally intensified by the reports from the North respecting the latest military operations of the German columns, which are certainly hard to reconcile with the pious opinions unanimously expressed at a special conference of the generals, held just before I left Peking, in favour of the partial withdrawal of the international forces at the earliest possible date. To perpetuate unrest and extend the area of administrative chaos by desultory expeditions which exasperate but cannot overawe, and at the same time to demand payment from China at an exorbitant rate for the maintenance of the troops engaged in these unworthy operations, is a policy diametrically opposed to the principles enunciated by Lord Lansdowne in the House of Lords.

Internal Reform

The necessity of reform is unquestionably more widely recognized among the Chinese themselves to-day than at any previous period, but reform cannot be initiated with an absolutely depleted treasury. Lord Lansdowne stated in the House of Lords that internal reforms are none of our business, but it must be hoped that this statement does not represent the last word of the British Government. Past experience surely has demonstrated how closely all questions of foreign intercourse with China are bound up with questions of internal reform. Had our influence during our 30 years' ascendancy in Peking been applied with more foresight and energy to promoting internal reforms China would have never sunk to her present condition of decay, fraught with such grave international perils. Again, if the British Government had shown a more intelligent appreciation of the real meaning of the *coup d'Etat* of 1898, instead of dismissing it as an internal question which was none of our business, we should not have had to deal to-day with such a legacy of disasters as the triumph of the reactionary party left behind it. Internal reforms are not the business of those Powers which desire for their own purposes to see the present condition of chaos prolonged, but they are essentially the business of the Powers which desire to see China restored to normal conditions of vitality.

Punishment

"An eye for an eye" was the attitude of the British public and government, outraged by the Chinese massacres of missionaries and others during 1900.

The Times, 10 September.

As one of the two edicts which the Chinese kept back to the last sanctions the punishment of the most guilty and prominent of the provincial officials who took part in the massacres, we trust that a strenuous attempt will now be made to secure the adequate and speedy chastisement of the miscreants responsible for the abominable outrages perpetrated at Chu-chau. The story of that hideous crime is well known, but the British public seem hardly to realize that the highly-placed magistrates who are the most culpable of the criminals have so far escaped scot free. Had

Throughout the summer of 1901, public beheadings of leaders responsible for the Boxer rising were carried out by Chinese acting under orders from the occupying Powers.

Mansell

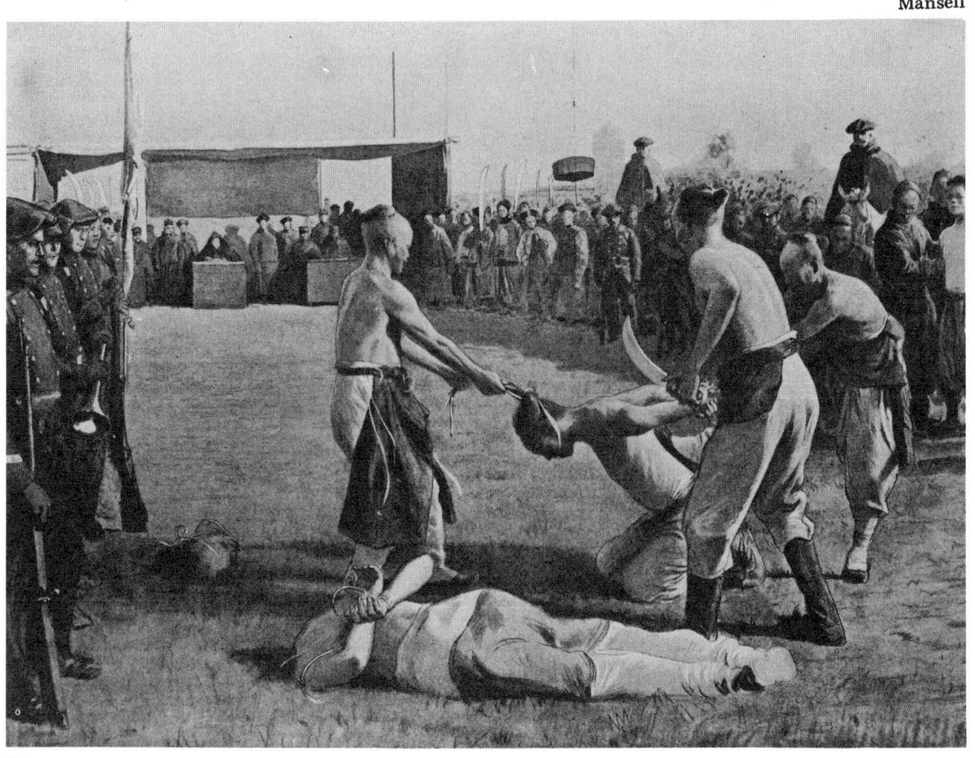

Mr. Warren been properly supported by the Foreign Office, they would have paid the penalty of their misdeeds early in the year. But, lest the British Government should incur any suspicion of acting outside the concert, the matter was taken out of his hands and referred to the Ministers at Peking. As one of those Ministers represented a Power which has acknowledged officially that she is not interested in the murder of missionaries, not much progress was to be expected. Not much has been made; for, only a few days ago, our Shanghai Correspondent reported that Yung-ching, the Provincial Treasurer, and Pao, the Taotai, who were the prime authors of the murders, had left Hang-chau without experiencing any tokens of Imperial displeasure. The Governor had beheaded a subordinate officer, and seems to have expressed his willingness to oblige us with two dozen of other heads. We want to convince him and his fellows that this is not the sort of satisfaction we will accept for the blood of our fellow-countrymen. We require the effective punishment of the real criminals—the criminals of high rank—and all who do not share Count Lamsdorff's sentiments towards missionaries expect the Government to spare no effort to secure it.

Expiation

The Times, 3 December.

In briefly noting the course of foreign affairs during 1901, it is right to give the first place to the Chinese question, which, a year ago, had brought together the forces of Europe, Japan, and the United States in a joint expedition, full of the seeds of possible danger. Although no man can say that the objects of that expedition were wholly gained, it is at least satisfactory to be able to record its peaceful termination, the return of all the troops except such as are necessary to guard the newly-fortified Legations and the way to the sea, and China's consent to pay a large indemnity amounting to 450,000,000 taels. Count Waldersee left for home on June 3, was received with great distinction by the Emperor William, and made—so his countrymen thought—too many speeches. Nor was unmixed satisfaction to be derived from the solemn " mission of expiation," undertaken by Prince Chun, the Emperor's brother, to the Court of Berlin, by way of doing penance for the murder of Baron von Ketteler; it was mismanaged, and the Chinese Court came out of the affair not perceptibly humiliated.

Reprisals

The Times, 21 December.

Punctually to the day fixed by the Imperial edict of November 30, the Chinese Court left Kai-fong-fu a week ago on its progress back to Peking. The step may prove to be of considerable importance in the history of the dynasty and of the State. It is, as our well-informed Shanghai Correspondent observes, a sign, so far as it goes, that the Throne is no longer unwilling to hearken to the counsels of responsible statesmen. The most patriotic and disinterested of the Mandarins, with the most intelligent appreciation of the real relations of their country to foreign Powers, have urged the adoption of this course, and the measure of success they have attained ought to strengthen their hands for the future. A still more significant indication of a change of sentiment, and, it may be, of a permanent change of policy in the highest quarters, is the disinheritance of the Heir-Apparent which was announced on the same day as that on which the departure of the Court from Kai-fong-fu was made public. It will be just two years ago next month since the Empress Dowager, in the plenitude of the power she had secured to herself by the overthrow of the reform projects adopted by the reigning Emperor in the autumn of 1898, and by the resumption of the regency, carried out a further palace revolution within the then mysterious recesses of the Pink Forbidden City. The Emperor Kwang Hsu, who had been confined to an island within the palace walls since his ill-starred attempt to assert his independence by countenancing Kang Yu-wei's schemes of reform, was induced to issue an edict nominating as his successor the son of Prince Tuan, who assumed the name of Pu Chun. This selection possessed a special and a sinister significance which did not at the time escape intelligent observers of Chinese affairs, though it made little impression on Peking diplomatists. Prince Tuan was notoriously qualified by his ignorance, his arrogance, and his hatred of foreigners for the high place he held at the head of the extreme reactionary party. The nomination of his son to a position of such present dignity and such prospective importance as that of heir to the reigning Sovereign was generally and rightly regarded by such observers as a clear indication of the leanings and of the probable policy of the real ruler of China. The fact that the Yang-tsze Viceroys protested against it should not be forgotten. They placed upon it the same interpretations as the Europeans who know China best, and events, it need hardly be said, soon justified some of the worst fears cherished by both. In one respect only were the prognostications of evil caused by that incident unfulfilled. The Emperor Kwang Hsu was not removed by one of those mysterious maladies which visit the interiors of Oriental palaces, to make way for his successor. He still lives, and in a manner reigns, though whether he is still anything more than a helpless puppet in the hands of his masterful relative is more than doubtful.

The Empress Dowager

Prince Tuan, we are assured, receives the severest censure. He is charged in terms of reproach with the chief responsibility for the Boxer rising and for its deplorable results. The repudiation of his policy and the degradation of his son, if they are the acts of the Empress Dowager and if they are not shams of the class which play so large a part in Chinese affairs, are equivalent to a complete recantation upon her part of the principles upon which she steadily and ostentatiously based her conduct from the *coup d'Etat* of 1898 down to her flight from Peking. We can hardly remain long in doubt as to the sincerity of her present professions, should she continue to exercise power as she has done hitherto. The world will judge her by her acts and not by her words. If she has really turned her back on the reactionaries who so very nearly brought her and her House to ruin, she will honour and reward the men who not only warned her, but saved China, at the risk of their lives and fortunes, from the worst consequences her infatuation was calculated to produce. If she is guided by them in the difficult task which lies before her, and if she places in their hands the execution of the reforms they rightly regard as indispensable, we shall be justified in regarding her change of policy as sincere. If she neglects or seeks to injure the men who saved her and China in defiance of the explicit orders of the Court, we shall know that she is incorrigible and that the progressive sentiments expressed in the late edicts are not intended to have any practical results.

Famine and the indemnity

The situation which the Court will have to face, when it reaches Peking, will tax whatever statesmanship it may possess to the uttermost. The Boxers and the troops of the civilized Powers between them have left widespread devastation behind them in the north; and though, as Prince Ching has himself very properly testified in a letter which appears amongst the official correspondence published yesterday, the British troops did their best to preserve what was left in the Summer Palace after it was evacuated by the Russians, the Imperial exiles will find ample traces in their capital of the reprisals which their own criminal folly brought upon them. There is a famine of appalling proportions in Shen-si, and the extravagant amount of the indemnity on which some of the Powers insisted constitutes a crushing burden on the population of the entire Empire. The financial position alone, apart from the position of Manchuria and any other questions of an international character, presents a problem which will demand both ability and courage for its solution. The new taxation will in any case bear heavily, and in native eyes unjustly, on the populations of

"Ping Pong";

Or, "A Game that he DOES understand."

Punch

those provinces which kept the peace and maintained friendly relations with the foreigners, against the express commands of the Court that will be taxing them to atone for the misdeeds it sanctioned. The anti-foreign party are, of course, actively employed in making the best use of the weapon with which the short-sighted action of some of the Powers has armed them. They are going about amongst the people, whispering that the new taxes, whose pressure is felt by every coolie in the Empire, are being raised to buy off the foreigner, and they are asking what Chinamen are to think of the assurances and the pretensions of a civilization which preaches peace and good will, but wrings millions from unoffending labourers, artisans, and farmers for offences in which all the world knows they had no part.

Ping-pong was the newest craze of 1901.

The Chinese Settlement and After

Graphic, 20 June.

The snake of Chinese Reaction has been severely scotched, but it has not been killed, and it remains to be seen whether, with the Dowager Empress at the helm, and all her anti-foreign advisers still at large, the relations with the Outer Barbarians will become really friendly again. For a time, at least, peace is assured, for there can be no defiance of the Powers, and no preparations for a hostile policy while the great burden of debt which China has assumed remains undischarged. As for the international situation, the prospect is neither clearer nor more reassuring. The Manchurian Question has yet to be settled, and behind that question is the still more serious Korean problem. That Russia really intends to evacuate Manchuria no one believes. If she remains there will the other Powers, or any of them, require compensation for themselves? The probability is that the negotiations will be so prolonged, and the occupation so disguised, that no complication will arise in this form. It will be very different, however, when Russia begins to push further southward as she inevitably must. Without Korea her hold on Manchuria must always be a source of anxiety to her, for her communications between Vladivostok and Port Arthur are thereby cut. Korea is as necessary to her in Eastern Asia as was Finland in Northern Europe, while the Sea of Japan is another Black Sea to her, and the Korean Straits another Dardanelles. Here, then, are the elements of persistent unrest. However peaceful may be the outward aspect of things, the consciousness of an unstable situation must always haunt the Powers. In a word, the settlement in China has only got rid of a few immediate troubles. It has left the real Far Eastern Question unsolved.

Fleecing the Chinese

Graphic, 20 April.

If the telegraphed figures of the indemnity that it is proposed to ask China to pay are accurate, some of the representatives of European Christianity must have curiously little regard for common honesty. Japan and the United States and England seem to have fixed their demands at a fairly moderate level; the other Powers appear to be utilizing the present opportunity to try and squeeze all the money they can out of China. The biggest bills are presented by Germany and Russia, but the latter has already more than

Girls from China were exported by slave-dealers to Chinamen in San Francisco, despite attempts by the U.S. Government to ban the trade and by missionaries to rescue the girls.

Graphic

paid herself in advance by virtually annexing Manchuria, and the former remains comfortable in the possession of Kiauchau, which she seized upon the most paltry of excuses a few years ago. As that seizure was the beginning of the serious troubles that have since disturbed the peace of the Far East and caused infinite misery, destruction, and bloodshed, it may be questioned whether China has not a greater moral claim to an indemnity from Germany. In any case the Powers cannot honestly hold themselves entirely blameless for the Boxer outbreak. Europe pressed her missionaries upon China against the wish of the Government and the people, while all the larger European Powers have annexed pieces of Chinese territory with entire disregard for international law. Our own record is little better than that of the rest, for we annexed the hinterland of Hong Kong without giving China any equivalent return for this valuable cession. The total bill that the Powers now present is said to amount to about 60,000,000*l*, and the experts are all discussing how China is to pay it. She cannot, of course, produce that amount in ready money, and it is not easy to see what sufficiently good security she can offer for a loan. The suggestion that the *likin* should be abolished, or reformed, has properly been rejected by Lord Lansdowne. It may be a very bad tax, but it is the main staple on which the local officials depend for their administrative work and for their own salaries. Europe simply does not possess the means to compel China to carry out such a revolutionary change as the abolition of *likin*, or its transference to European collectors. The only other definite suggestion is the increase of the Customs duties; but unless this increase were accomplished by an internal Excise, which is practically impossible, the effect would be to further encourage the setting up of Chinese mills to the disadvantage of Lancashire and of German and American manufacturers. As these essential difficulties come to be faced, it is probable that the Powers, in their own interest, will consent to abate their demands, and to write off part of their losses as a bad debt.

Russia in Manchuria

To the dismay of other powers with interests there, Manchuria was coming under Russian domination. Russia had already leased Port Arthur (now Lushun) from the Chinese (to use as an ice-free naval base, strategically near Peking—and Japan); and in 1901 she connected her Trans-Siberian Railway to it. Germany was reluctant to join Britain in opposing Russia's further encroachments in Manchuria (which fact contributed to the worsening of Anglo-German relations), but Japan was more than eager to do so. However, China herself, afraid of offending the other powers, withdrew from negotiating with Russia over Manchuria.

A Manchurian Agreement

The Times, 3 Jan. This was a " scoop ". Even the Empress of China had not known of the agreement until she read about it in The Times.

An agreement has been concluded between Russia and China regarding the Russian military occupation of Feng-tien, the southern and most important part of Manchuria, and the resumption of Chinese civil administration under Russian protection. The agreement was signed by representatives of Tseng, the Tartar General at Mukden, and General Korostovitch, representing Admiral Alexeiff, the Russian Commander-in-Chief. Russia consents to allow the Tartar General and the Chinese officials to resume the civil government of Mukden and Feng-tien province on the following conditions:

1. The Tartar General Tseng undertakes to protect the province and pacify it, and to assist in the construction of the railroad.
2. He must treat kindly the Russians in military occupation, protecting the railway and pacifying the province, and provide them with lodgings and provisions.
3. He must disarm and disband the Chinese soldiery, delivering in their entirety to the

Russian military officials all munitions of war in their arsenals not already occupied by the Russians.

4. All forts and defences in Feng-tien not occupied by the Russians, and all powder magazines not required by the Russians, must be dismantled in the presence of Russian officials.

5. Nin-chwang and other places now occupied by the Russians shall be restored to the Chinese civil administration when the Russian government is satisfied that the pacification of the province is complete.

6. The Chinese shall maintain law and order by local police under the Tartar General.

7. A Russian political Resident with general powers of control shall be stationed at Mukden, to whom the Tartar General must give all information respecting any important measure.

8. Should the local police be insufficient in any emergency, the Tartar General will communicate with the Russian Resident at Mukden and invite Russia to despatch reinforcements.

9. The Russian text shall be standard.

The functions given to the Russian Resident are similar to those of the Russian Resident at Bokhara or of the British Residents in the Native States in India.

The agreement will necessarily be followed by similar agreements with reference to the other two provinces, and then Manchuria will be a *de facto* Russian protectorate, Russia, by a pre-existing agreement, having already the right to maintain all necessary troops for the protection of the railway.

The Manchurian Danger

Graphic, 9 March

There can be no doubt that a very serious turn has been given to the Far Eastern Crisis by the action of Russia in regard to Manchuria. It will be remembered that some six weeks ago information was received of an Agreement concluded by Admiral Alexeieff, in virtue of which what seemed to be a Russian Protectorate was sought to be established over Manchuria. We expressed the opinion at the time that the import of that Agreement had been exaggerated, and our view was confirmed by assurances given by the Russian Government to the effect that the Agreement was purely military and provisional, and that nothing in the nature of annexation was contemplated. Since then rumours of a further Treaty have reached London through the medium, as usual, of Dr. Morrison, the wonderfully well-informed Peking correspondent of the *Times.* This Treaty is clearly neither military nor provisional, and, although the Russian Government complains that it has been divulged in a mutilated form, none of its essential provisions has been repudiated. That this instrument is intended to establish a virtual Russian Protectorate in Manchuria, and at the same time to extinguish important rights now enjoyed by foreigners in that province, is incontestable, and it has consequently led to protests, which have been lodged against it with the Chinese Government by no fewer than six of the Powers. Under these circumstances, we do not believe for a moment that it will be persisted in; but it is, nevertheless, a very alarming incident. In the first place, it is clearly an act of bad faith on the part of Russia, since it is in contravention of her own expressed desire that the Powers should act in concert in China, and that their action should be primarily directed to the preservation of the integrity of the Middle Kingdom. But this is not its most disturbing aspect. That one of these days Russia would endeavour to acquire Manchuria everybody has known, and it has been equally understood that when that day arrived there would be a serious crisis. It now seems that Russia is not disposed to postpone the attempt indefinitely, and if it is withdrawn now we may expect to see it revived very shortly again in another form. Whenever it is revived, it will, we fear, prove the signal for a disastrous scramble for Chinese territory. Japan is not likely to allow Russia to settle

QUITE AT HOME.

BRITISH AND GERMAN ALLIES. "HI! WHAT ARE YOU DOING THERE?"
RUSSIAN COSSACK. "I'M THE MAN IN POSSESSION! ARE YOU GOING TO TURN ME OUT?"
BOTH (*hesitating*). "N—N—NO. NO. WE ONLY ASKED."
RUSSIAN COSSACK. "THEN NOW YOU KNOW." [*Goes on smoking.*

Punch/Mansell

herself in Manchuria without demanding compensation. Indeed she has already made it clear that she would do so. The action of Japan would inevitably lead to similar action on the part of the other Powers, and such action could not possibly take place without a collision between some of them. These are the grave possibilities opened by the action of Russia. We trust most earnestly that the Powers will deal with it in such a way as to avert these possibilities. A wise statesmanship will endeavour to arrange a friendly understanding by which the essential aims and interests of all the Powers may be permanently safeguarded. Instead of crying " Hands off " to Russia we shall do well to endeavour to find a way of meeting her wishes without injuring the interests of any other Power. It is useless to wrangle about the ethics of the transaction. What is wanted is a frank interchange of views. Unfortunately frankness is not a Russian characteristic.

Inability to Sign

The Times, 5 April.

China, in her notification to Russia announcing her inability to sign the Manchurian Convention, says it is her desire to keep on friendly terms with all nations. She declares that she is at present going through the most perilous period in the history of the Empire, and that it is therefore necessary to have the friendship of all. However much she might be willing, it would be impossible to grant any special privilege to one Power when the others objected for the sake of obtaining the friendship of one by alienating the sympathy of all.

An Ally at Sea

A major change in Britain's foreign policies took place during 1901. Foreign Secretary Lord Lansdowne's thinking increasingly moved away from the isolationist policy of the past, which could only be sustained if Britain's navy exceeded those of any two potential allies against her. As the other powers' navies grew bigger and bigger, it was impossible to achieve this aim. Instead, alliances were necessary, so that the navy's resources need not be spread thinly world wide but concentrated where most needed. This change of outlook was expressed in Lansdowne's dealings with Japan, and with America, during 1901.

Japan, although now becoming a significant military power, feared Russia's encroachments in nearby Manchuria *(see page 62)* *in which France and Germany acquiesced. Britain, too, was anxious to maintain the* status quo *in the Far East; was not friendly with France or Russia; and, as 1901 wore on, was abandoning all thought of alliance with Germany. Japan therefore saw in her a likely ally—though where Japan was intent on a showdown with Russia, Britain wanted peace.*

The Anglo-Japanese negotiations, leading to a treaty in January, 1902, were kept secret from Parliament and Press during 1901.

A Question of Size

A secret cabinet memorandum by Selborne, First Lord of the Admiralty, 17 January.

Hitherto, the policy of this country has been stated to be so to build battle-ships as to maintain an equality of numbers with the combined battle-ships of the two Powers possessing for the moment the largest fleets. It does not seem to me that this basis of calculation is one that will any longer serve, considering that within the last five years three new navies have sprung into existence —those of the United States, Germany, and Japan. It is certain that it would be a hopeless task to attempt to achieve an equality with the three largest navies; but I go further, and say that, if the United States continue their present naval policy and develop their navy as they are easily capable of developing it if they choose, it will be scarcely possible for us to raise our navy to a strength equal to that both of France and of the United States combined. I propose therefore to consider our position almost exclusively from its relative strength to that of France and Russia combined, and from that point of view it seems to me that what we should aim at is, not a numerical equality, but a strength drawn partly from numbers but largely also from superiority of ships armaments crews and training, such as will enable us to have a reasonable expectation of beating France and Russia, if ever unfortunately we should find ourselves engaged in a war with them.

Balance of Naval Power in the Far East

Cabinet Memorandum, by Selborne, 4 September.

The recognized standard for the naval strength of Great Britain has hitherto been equality with the ships of the two next greatest naval Powers.

I have already given to the Cabinet my reasons for thinking that this standard would be beyond the strength of this country if the United States were to use all their resources to develop their naval strength, and that it is inadequate if applied to a possible war against France in alliance with Russia.

For us victory in such a war is a condition of continued existence as an Empire. To

Japanese battleship Mikasa *awaiting action.*

Imperial War Museum

them, defeat would bring no corresponding consequences. Accordingly it appears to me to be running too grave a risk to be content to enter upon a contest with two such Powers on terms of simple equality of strength.

In considering, however, the value to this country of some sort of naval alliance with Japan I will deal with the question from the point of view of our position in a war with France and Russia in which we started with an equality, but without any superiority, of strength in battleships.

The decisive battles in such a war would certainly be fought in European waters; but it does not follow that we should be free to concentrate the whole of our naval strength in those waters and leave the outlying parts of the Empire to await the final issue.

I am strongly in favour of concentrating our strength, as far as possible, at the spot at which the final issue will be fought out; but some risks would be too great to run even for this object.

The case of Far Eastern seas strikingly illustrates what I mean.

If the British Navy were defeated in the Mediterranean and the Channel the stress of our position would not be alleviated by any amount of superiority in the Chinese seas. If, on the other hand, it were to prove supreme in the Mediterranean and Channel, even serious disasters in Chinese seas would matter little. These considerations furnish, therefore, a sound argument for keeping our naval strength in Chinese waters as low as is compatible with the safety of the Empire. But there is a point below which it would be dangerous to go. It is true that victory in European waters would scarcely be dimmed by even serious disasters in the Far East, but its value though not obliterated would be impaired to a dangerous degree if British naval power in the Far East were crushed out of existence. We could afford to lose a certain number of merchantmen, or even to see a weaker squadron of battleships blockaded for a time in Hong Kong; but we could not afford to see our Chinese trade disappear, or to see Hong Kong and Singapore fall, particularly not at a moment when a military struggle with Russia might be in progress on the confines of India.

At the present moment the naval position in the Far East is changing. Russia has increased, and is still largely adding to, the strength of what used to be her Baltic Squadron; but the whole of that squadron practically has been transferred from Cronstadt to Vladivostock and Port Arthur. Dealing only with battleships and cruisers, the present relative naval strength in Far Eastern seas is as seen in the table below.

Russia has eleven battle-ships and rather more cruisers of various classes now building, of which three battle-ships and four cruisers (among those on the actual eve of completion) will, it is believed, be shortly added to her fleet in the Far East.

Japan has one more battle-ship nearly ready. Otherwise she has only two cruisers now building.

From these figures it will be seen that in a few months' time Great Britain will have four first-class battle-ships and sixteen cruisers in Chinese waters as against a combined French and Russian strength of seven first-class and two second-class battle-ships and twenty cruisers. It is highly improbable that France will increase her strength in those seas; her naval policy is as far as possible one of concentration in the Mediterranean and Channel, but especially in the Mediterranean.

	France	Russia.	Great Britain.	Japan.
Battle-ships	1 (2nd Class)	5 (1—2nd Class)	4	6 (1—2nd Class)
Cruisers				
1st Class Armoured	2 (old type)	6	3 (2 old type and " Cressy ")	7 (6 new)
1st Class Protected	2		4	
2nd Class	5	1	8	10
3rd Class			1	14

For us the odds of nine battle-ships to four would be too great, and we should have eventually to add to our battle-ships on the China Station. The effect of this would be twofold. It would leave us with little or nothing more than a bare equality of strength in the Channel and Mediterranean, and bare equality at the heart of the Empire is a dangerous risk. It would strain our naval system greatly, and would add to our expenditure on the manning of the Navy. Every ship on the China Station must be kept in commission, and be fully manned in time of peace; for this purpose the naval reserves are never available, and special additions would have to be made to the establishment of active service ratings. Some of the cruisers also on the China Station are badly needed elsewhere. The case would bear a different aspect were we assured of the alliance of Japan.

Great Britain and Japan together would next year be able to show eleven battle-ships against the French and Russian nine, as well as a preponderance of cruisers.

Great Britain would be under no necessity of adding to the number of battle-ships on the China Station, and at last would be in a position to contemplate the possibility of shortly establishing a small margin of superiority in reserve at home; the number of our cruisers could be reduced on that station, and increased on other stations where badly required; our Far Eastern trade and possessions would be secure.

Japan, on the other hand, would be delivered from the nightmare of seeing her rising power crushed by the combination of the French and Russian fleets.

The form which the proposed alliance or understanding might take would be somewhat of this sort: Great Britain might engage herself to come to the assistance of Japan, if in a quarrel between Japan and Russia France came to the assistance of Russia, or *vice versâ*. Japan might engage herself to come to the assistance of Great Britain, if in a quarrel between Great Britain and France Russia came to the assistance of France, or *vice versâ*.

Such an agreement would, I believe, add materially to the naval strength of this country all over the world, and effectively diminish the probability of a naval war with France or Russia singly or in combination.

The United States A new Ally

The Hay-Pauncefote Treaty concluded late in 1901 has been called one of the great treaties of the twentieth century, and Lansdowne's biggest achievement as Foreign Secretary.

Its significance was that it marked a complete change in Anglo-U.S. relations, hitherto so precarious that Britain always had contingency plans for war with the U.S. at the ready. Under the treaty, Britain allowed America virtual control of the vital new link between Atlantic and Pacific, and left peace in the Caribbean in her custody. This was part of Lansdowne's new policy of alliances in areas from which the British navy could then be withdrawn to concentrate elsewhere *(see page 65)**.*

The treaty (named after American Foreign Secretary Hay and British Ambassador Pauncefote) allowed America the sole right to fortify the projected canal provided she guaranteed to keep it open to all users, whether in war or in peace.

The Hay-Pauncefote Treaty Signed

The Times, 19 November.

The new treaty gives the United States sole authority and control over the canal, makes this Government the sole guarantor of neutrality, and secures England equal commercial rights in the use of the canal. England undoubtedly waives certain objections she has heretofore pressed, but this waiver is the result, not of dictation, but of negotiations ending in the final and complete agreement of the two Govern-

Graphic

The canal treaty—crucial to the balance of power in the Pacific—was debated by U.S. Senators on the Committee on Foreign Relations, meeting in the Capitol.

ments on all points. There is no disposition on the part of this Government to claim the result as a triumph or regard it as a surrender by England. The right to protect the canal is considered to grow out of the exclusive guarantee by the United States.

Every view I have heard expressed in Washington in the highest quarters is one of rejoicing over the good understanding between the two countries. While it is not thought that England has relinquished anything of value to her, it is felt that the United States gains a free hand in building a canal which she must have for the peaceful development of her maritime resources.

Great Britain Withdraws

Washington, November 18.

The new Hay-Pauncefote Canal Treaty was signed by Mr. Hay and Lord Pauncefote at five minutes past 12 today.

The principal point of difference between the new treaty and the one that failed to pass the Senate is the withdrawal of Great Britain from the joint guarantee of the neutrality of the canal, leaving the United States as sole guarantor. The section of the old provision respecting the right to fortify the canal leaves that right by inference with the United States. All commerce, of whatever nationality, will fare alike.

American millionaires agree to purchase the Leyland Line (Mediterranean, Portugal, Montreal and Antwerp) Fleets.

John Bull: 'Now, my little man, what can I do for you?'

Master Jonathan: 'Wal, guess I'll buy the whole store!'

Punch

Giant of Steel

With the rapid advance of U.S. industries came the spread of the huge corporations (' trusts ') against which Theodore Roosevelt was to fight, even though it was his party (the Republicans) which had the support of big business. In 1901 J. Pierpont Morgan's U.S. Steel Corporation was launched, with assets equalling the entire revenue of Britain. In the newer industries—steel, electrical, motor and chemical—both America and Germany were now fast outstripping Britain.

Momentous Events in the U.S.

The Times, 31 December.

Several events of moment, commercial and political, have marked the history of the United States during the year. In February the world was startled by the news of the most gigantic " deal " ever known; the purchase of the Carnegie Steel Company and six similar concerns by a trust or syndicate with Mr. Pierpont Morgan at its head, the capital of the new trust amounting to more than £200,000,000 sterling. One incidental result of this was that a few months later Mr. Carnegie handed over to a body of trustees the sum of two millions sterling as an endowment for the Universities of his native Scotland. A less agreeable consequence of the feverish speculation caused by this and other " deals " was a great panic, which took place in May, on the New York Stock Market; but affairs righted themselves more quickly than usual.

£8,000,000 A YEAR PROFIT

The Marvellous Organisation by which the Carnegie Works Supply the World with American Steel

Daily Express, 2 January.

In 1855 Great Britain made about 50,000 tons of steel—a very slight advance on the 35,000 tons which was the annual output at the beginning of the century. The year marked an epoch, because in that year the Bessemer process was patented. In the course of a dozen years more the Siemens process came into rivalry with it.

Within forty-five years—dating from Bessemer's patent—the British steel trade has grown so marvellously that its output in 1899 was 4,855,325 tons—a grand total sufficient to build 440 vessels like the Oceanic! Moreover, our annual production increases. We made more steel last year by 289,339 tons than we did in the year previous—more by 2,316,075 tons than eleven years prior to that date.

Englishmen are proud of these big figures. But from across the Atlantic there looms the shadow of a vaster steel industry, which most seriously menaces our own, and the strength of which has been altogether unsuspected until within the last few years.

In that country, where labour is better paid than it is here, a grand total of 10,639,857 tons of steel was produced in 1899, 5,784,532 tons in excess of our own—considerably more than double, in fact! So that our own growth has not been in anything like the same ratio as that of our rivals.

The Steel Invasion of England

During the great strike of three years ago Messrs. Harland and Wolff, of Belfast—threatened with boycott by the English makers—imported some American steel for shipbuilding. To-day the material is coming over in increasing quantities, under-selling the product of the Scotch furnaces on the Clyde. It is used in the building of British ships: so-called British steel is manufactured from American " blooms " and " billets "—trade terms applied to the rectangular blocks from which thin plates are rolled.

England's natural resources having been drawn upon heavily, those of America are as good as undeveloped. It is unfavourable to Britain that her coal becomes more difficult to mine. It is all in favour of the United States that her coalfields are nearly virgin areas. Coal lies in abundance in Pennsylvania, the Virginias, North Carolina, Maryland, Tennessee, Georgia, and Alabama. In Western Pennsylvania alone it is estimated that enough coal lies above the water level to supply the wants of the States for 500 years!

The Only Remedy

The statement of these leading facts should indicate the only way in which the lost supremacy of Britain may possibly be reasserted.

If English firms will use some of their big profits in laying down modern plant and reorganising their methods there will be some hope for the future. Much of the plant in use here is twenty years old or more—a long period as things move now. In steel-making, as in some departments of engineering practice, machinery should be superannuated within from five to ten years, and it is so treated in some few live shops.

ASSASSINATION

The wave of migrants from south and central Europe at this period brought with it some anarchistic traditions which were to be inflamed by the exploitation of labour in America. The educational philanthropies of millionaires like Rockefeller and Carnegie did not reconcile the masses to their lot. McKinley's assassination by Czolgosz led to his Vice-President becoming the youngest President ever: Theodore Roosevelt, monopoly-buster, practical reformer and friend of Britain—a change with immense effects in history.

Mr. McKinley Shot

The Times, 7 September.

Mr. McKinley has been shot at the Academy of Music, Buffalo, by a stranger. Two shots took effect in the stomach.

The President's condition is serious.

5 p.m.

President McKinley was shot by a well-dressed man while holding a reception in the Academy of Music. The man was one of those who shook hands with him. He shook hands with one hand, and fired the shots with the other. The assailant was arrested.

As soon as the news was known in New York steps were taken to call a meeting of the great commercial interests to devise measures to protect the stock market.

5.15 p.m.

Mr. McKinley is resting easily. He is conscious.

Later.

Mr. McKinley's assailant is a man named Fred Nieman, said to be from Detroit. He has resided in Buffalo a week. He says he is of Polish nationality, and admits that he is an Anarchist.

7.40 p.m.

I am now able to send the following connected account of the attempt to murder Mr. McKinley to-day.

While the President was receiving in the Temple of Music at Buffalo this afternoon he was approached by a well-dressed man wearing a silk hat, who had one hand covered with a handkerchief. As the man extended his hand to the President, apparently in order to shake hands, he fired a shot, which entered the President's right breast, lodging against the breastbone. Immediately afterwards the man fired another shot, which entered the abdomen.

Quick as a flash a score of men threw themselves upon the assailant. Cries of "Lynch him" were heard on every hand; but the police managed to rescue the man, who was covered with blood from a gash in the face. He was taken to the station house near the Pan-American Exposition grounds and afterwards to the police headquarters.

When he was shot the President fell into the arms of Detective Geary. "Am I shot?" he asked. The detective opened his vest, and, on seeing blood, replied, "Yes, I am afraid you are, Mr. President."

Mr. McKinley was at once taken to the Emergency Hospital, where the bullet, which had lodged against the breast-bone, was removed at 6 o'clock. Dr. Russell Roswell Parke, the well-known surgeon, arrived, and, after putting the President under the influence of an anaesthetic, began probing for the bullet in the abdomen. He tried for some time, but, not being successful, sewed the wound up. The physicians say that, while the wounds are serious, they need not necessarily be fatal. The chief operator at the White House has received a message saying that it is believed that the President will live.

When examined at the police headquarters, the prisoner said he was Fred Nieman, of Detroit. When asked why he committed the deed he said :—"I am an Anarchist, and have done my duty." Later he denied that he was an Anarchist.

The public of New York were absolutely stunned by the news. At first few believed it to be true. They could not conceive that even the most bigoted Anarchist could wish to harm President McKinley.

At this hour Newspaper Row is crowded with anxious people awaiting the latest bulletins. Similar scenes are reported from Washington.

Buffalo, September 6, 5.14 p.m.

A bullet which had lodged against the breast has been extracted, and the President continues to rest easy.

6 p.m.

Mrs. McKinley has not yet heard of the attempt on her husband.

Dr. Parker, a prominent physician, is now probing for the bullet lodged in the abdomen.

Police Commissioner Cooper has had a conversation with Nieman, who then denied being an Anarchist. Nieman fired through a handkerchief in which he had concealed his weapon. Detective Ireland, who was only 2ft. away, immediately jumped upon him and brought him to the ground. In an instant 20 other men precipitated themselves upon him, and when Nieman was rescued from their hands he had his face cut open and was covered with blood. He is now locked up at the police headquarters.

6.30 p.m.

A physician who left the hospital a few minutes before 6 reports that the respiration of the patient is easy and the pulse good. An anaesthetic had been administered and the probing for the second bullet had begun.

When shot, the President fell into the arms of Detective Geary, to whom he coolly said: "Am I shot?" The detective unbuttoned his vest, and, seeing blood, replied: "I am afraid you are, Mr. President."

It is now stated that soon after the outrage Nieman, on being asked why he shot the President, replied, "I am an Anarchist, I did my duty."

7 p.m.

At 6.50 the physicians announced that while the President's wounds were serious they were not necessarily fatal. The bullet in the abdomen has not yet been found, but the wound has been sewn up. The President was then recovering from the effects of the chloroform.

Buffalo, September 6.

President McKinley at the time of the attack was surrounded by a cordon of police, and his assailant was promptly captured without any resistance. The prisoner had to be guarded closely to prevent the people from lynching him.

It is believed that the wounds will not

prove fatal, although they are extremely dangerous.

The best physicians of Buffalo as well as the President's family doctor are now at his bedside.

The police were at first afraid to remove the prisoner owing to the threatening attitude of the people, but subsequently they transferred him safely to the police headquarters, where he revealed his identity.

One of Mr. McKinley's police escort said that the shots were fired at the public reception at the Temple of Music, not at the Ethnology building. " Nieman was in line with the other spectators," continued this police officer, " and approached the President with a cloth over one hand. He succeeded in getting close to the President, because no more notice was taken of him than of the others. The first thing the police knew was that he had fired two shots."

7.30 p.m.

The second bullet has just been successfully extracted. The first bullet fell from the wound in the breast-bone as soon as the President was placed on the operating table. Mr. McKinley picked it up himself and handed it to the doctor standing at his side. No anaesthetics were applied to the President when the surgeons probed for the second bullet. Immediately after it was removed there were marked signs of improvement. The President lies at the Emergency Hospital.

New York, September 6.

President McKinley is now in a hospital in the Exhibition grounds. His condition is serious.

Later.

The President was shot in front of the Ethnology buildings on his way to the Temple of Music.

He is fatally injured; one shot passed through the left breast, and the other entered the abdomen.

6 p.m.

Colonel Roosevelt, the Vice-President, who is in Vermont, is due to arrive at Burlington at 7 o'clock. The news was conveyed to him by telephone.

Cleveland, Ohio, September 6.

Senator Hanna, on hearing of the attempted assassination of President McKinley, became prostrated and exclaimed : " My God ! It cannot be possible. It is terrible. I am too shocked to express my feelings."

Detroit, September 6.

Mr. Alger, when apprised of the attempt on the life of the President, completely broke down, and tears streamed down his face.

The Lynching Scene

Morning Leader, 17 September.

The *New York Journal* gives a graphic suggestion of the manner in which the assassin concealed his weapon in an apparently bandaged hand.

Again, the *Journal* prints in diagram form these three scenes of the shooting; first picture showing the assailant approaching the President; the second showing how the two shots were fired; the third showing where the shots struck the President and his attitude after the shooting. This is how the *Journal* correspondent describes the scene.

Those at the back of the President " saw a small, dark, well-dressed young man, with what seemed to be a bandage about his right hand, extend his left to the President, and as he reached to take it the supposed bandage fell, there was the gleam of a weapon, a flash of fire. The smile on the President's face disappeared. A negro shouted and threw himself upon the dark man, but before he could close the second shot was fired. The President's outstretched hand fell, and he dropped back into the chair."

The assassination. Morning Leader

The same paper illustrates, " from description," the attempt to lynch Czolgosz: " Those near Mr. McKinley surged to him," it says. " Those outside the stand fell upon the man with a revolver. There was little noise; just a muffle of blows that fell too thickly to do much hurt, and a scuffling andgrowling of men who meant to kill. The intentness and unanimity of the purpose to have the life of the man who had shot the nation's head saved him. Too many were striking at him with fists and feet for it to be possible for any serious blow to reach him.

" The pressure of the crowd was so great that he could not even fall, else he would have been stamped to death then and there. . . . The confusion was only for a moment. The police awoke to the situation in an instant, and in a solid phalanx wedged their way to the squirming nucleus of the writhing crowd. A policeman got a hand on the collar of the President's assailant and jerked him from the ruck of people. He was swallowed up in a solid block of policemen, upon which the surging waves of frenzied people broke in vain."

Morning Leader

Well served by poets and novelists —Thomas Hardy (1) and Rudyard Kipling (2) and wits such as Max Beerbohm (7)—the arts scene was weak in artists, although Sargent was still painting. From the Continent, Alphonse Mucha influenced graphic design (11). The wave of library and museum building continued with the Horniman Museum (6) by Harrison Townsend. Music was in a doldrums relieved by the work of Sir Edward Elgar (3). Music hall artists—George Robey as 'The Tramp' (4), Harry Lauder (9) and Marie Lloyd (10)—flourished, and the 'legitimate' theatre was rich in such names as Sarah Bernhardt (5).

des
XXme
SITION
CENT
1896
0·50
11
8
10
9
Mr. Fred Story and Miss Ruth Devonport
"THE GAY CITY" AT THE ALHAMBRA

Workers Struggle

Over a million workers were now organized in trade unions, and as mechanization and the size of companies increased so did strikes (most of them unsuccessful), though they were fewer and less violent than in America and some European countries. There was no Ministry of Labour yet, and unemployment was still not seen as a political issue.

When the House of Lords ruled in 1901 that the striking union must compensate the Taff Vale Railway Company for profits lost (£30,000), this made striking too costly a risk for most unions to take. (The situation was reversed in 1906, by Act of Parliament).

Indignation at the Taff Vale judgment was instrumental in the workers' seeking to get themselves properly represented in Parliament (there were only two Labour MPs at the time, and only two adults out of three had a vote) and this accelerated the formation of the Parliamentary Labour Party.

The Taff Vale Case

The Times, 23 July.

The judgment delivered by the House of Lords yesterday in the " Taff Vale Railway Company *v.* Amalgamated Society of Railway Servants and others " is of far-reaching importance to the whole community. Their Lordships have unanimously held that a trade union registered under the Trade Union Acts can be sued in its registered name, and that the remarkable judgment given by Mr. Justice Farwell in September last and reversed in November must be restored. The decision is in accordance with the principles of common sense and common justice which we have long contended should apply to the powerful associations that exercise so vast a power over the labour market and through it over the industries of the country.

Lord Chancellor Concurs

Admitting the weight of the contentions advanced by the Master of the Rolls in the judgment which has now been set aside, we ventured to suggest, in our comments on the appeal from Mr. Justice Farwell, that possibly the House of Lords might dissent from the view adopted by that eminent lawyer and his colleagues. The dissent is in all material respects complete. The Lord Chancellor has declared himself content to adopt the judgment of Mr. Justice Farwell. He has expressed his entire concurrence in it and his inability to find any satisfactory answer to it in the decision which overruled it. " If," he said, " the Legislature has created a thing which can own property, which can employ servants, which can inflict injury, it must be taken, I think to have impliedly given the power to make it suable in a Court of law for injuries purposely done by its authority and procurement." That is merely a re-statement of the broad principle underlying Mr. Justice Farwell's judgment. The contention of the defendant society, he said, implied that " the Legislature had authorized the creation of numerous bodies of men, capable of owning great wealth and of acting by agents, with absolutely no responsibility for the wrongs they may do to other people by the use of that wealth and the employment of those agents." He refused to accept a contention which involved consequences so unjust and so dangerous, and the House of Lords have now declared that he was right.

This decision entirely alters in some material respects the privileged position which trade unions believed themselves to enjoy and were generally supposed to enjoy in this country. It deprives them of an immunity which has been often and grossly abused, and declares for the first time that they have neither greater nor less responsibilities before the law for the acts of their servants and agents than the rest of His Majesty's subjects. The principle it lays down has been bitterly denounced in advance in the dissent report signed by Mr. Abraham and other labour leaders who sat upon the Labour Commission; but, in spite of the interested opposition it is likely to meet, we believe it will commend itself to the natural sense of justice of the British people.

The Status of Trade Unions

Richard Bell was one of the three Labour MPs, and he was secretary of the railwaymen's trade union. The Clarion *was a weekly that circulated in the industrial north.*

House of Lords Decision
by Richard Bell, M.P.

Clarion, 3 August.

The Lords have given many important decisions from time to time affecting the working classes, but, in my opinion, never a decision affecting so many at one time and so far-reaching in its consequences as the one given last week in the appeal case, Taff Vale Railway *v.* A.S.R.S.

The appeal arose out of the strike which took place on that railway in August last year. The details leading up to it I need not enter into further than to say that it was organised and brought about without consultation with or sanction from the Executive Committee or responsible officials. But immediately after the men decided to strike they appealed to the Executive Committee for support. After considerable discussion and a division of opinion, the Executive Committee, by a majority of one, granted the request. The General Secretary, by virtue of his office, had then to take charge of it and conduct it through. The strike lasted a fortnight. During the progress of the dispute certain unlawful acts in picketing were alleged to have taken place, and upon these allegations the Company applied to an injunction against the A.S.R.S.—myself, as the General Secretary, and Mr. Holmes, Organising Secretary. It will be remembered that the Society appealed to have its name struck out, as it could not be sued. Justice Farwell decided against the Society. Appeal was then lodged in the Court of Appeal. The Master of the Rolls and his two colleagues reversed the decision. The Taff Vale Company then took it to the Lords, whose decision is now well known.

The decision is not one of what the law is, but what the Lords thought the law ought to be. We all agree that all legislation should be based upon common sense and justice, and, according to their Lordships' judgment, the position held by the Trade Unions till then was not based upon these two virtues. We must, therefore, say that up till now we enjoyed a privilege.

I have not always said popular things in connection with the Labour movement, and I have very often been the object of a good deal of unfair criticism, and sometimes abuse, for expressing my views and opinions as to the conduct of some sections of Trade Unionists, and what I am going to say now may not be popular.

Abuse of the Right to Strike

In reviewing the strikes that have taken place during recent years—say, the last five years—it will be found that the greatest number of them have been unauthorised by the respective Unions. They have generally been commenced by some section of the members, and the Executives afterwards appealed to for support, which invariably has been given.

This may rightly be termed as abusing the privilege enjoyed. I have many times said that such precipitated actions would, some day, certainly retaliate. That day has now come. It will be admitted by a good many that of recent years the rank and file have been running away with the Unions, rules, executive committees, and responsible officials of the Unions being entirely ignored. Strikes, started in many instances without sufficient consideration as to cause, and too often none as to the chance of success or consequences. A very large percentage of these strikes have been unsuccessful. The men gaining nothing, but losing a great deal, besides losses to employers and inconvenience to the public. The latter at any rate, being an item which cannot be ignored in these days.

Strikes under certain conditions were no doubt annoying to employers. They could see that irresponsible men brought about strikes whenever they choosed, and that the Executives seemed to have no control over their officials or members. Contracts between workmen and employers were often broken with impunity, and yet they had no remedy against the Unions so offending. This was a privilege enjoyed by the Unions for 30 years, and was well worthy of being more judiciously used. The increasing abuse of this privileged power has long been observed, by some of us, who have watched and studied the progress of the Labour movement, to be occupying the close and jealous attention of the Employers' Association, and they were determined to do all they could to deprive us of it. I know that if the decision of the Lords had been in our favour that effort at legislation in the same direction would be ,attempted next year. That is now unnecessary. The Unions, by this judge-made law, can now be made liable for damages caused by the action of their Executives or officials. Those who will feel the result most will be the industrial Jingoes, for we have, unfortunately, some who are as eager for strikes as other are for war.

Discipline and Education

To hope to get back to *status quo* will be positively in vain, and it would be a waste of time to think about it. What Trade Unionists must, therefore, do is to devote their attention and skill towards adapting themselves to the new situation, and provide themselves with the greatest protection for the future.

The members of the various Unions will have to see that they elect their strongest men on the Executives and the most level-headed men as their officials. The Executives must, in turn, insist upon the rules of the Societies being strictly adhered to. Strikes brought about by irresponsible officials or members must under no circumstances be countenanced, or they will become liable for damages caused thereby to the employers.

Members of Unions having grievances (and there are plenty) must refer them to the Executives; they may endeavour to negotiate for their redress. Failing satisfactory results, members and Executive, being convinced as to the genuineness of their claims, may decide upon a strike. Legal notices to terminate contracts must be given. The strike must then be conducted by a responsible official, for whose conduct and acts, if proved unlawful, the Union will be made liable for damages.

It, then, becomes absolutely necessary for the better training of discipline than we have hitherto seen in many of the Unions, and that the rank and file should respect more than they often do the governing bodies. Employers must, and probably will, respect the Unions in future more than they have hitherto done, being able to place more confidence in them that they can better control their members against precipitated strikes. Unless this will be done, compulsory arbitration must become more popular than it has up to now. If the employers will commence to take undue advantage of the position in which the Unions are now placed, they may depend upon retaliation. Over two millions of Trade Unionists, and the thousands of sympathetic Non-unionists, are not going to lie dormant and let their position be weakened and destroyed, Non-unionists will, and must see that their positions have been weakened in the same proportion as the Trade Unionists, and will, I have no doubt, join the Unions, and so strengthen them. The Unions must also arrange to protect their benefit funds from being used for strike purposes, and from being reached for damages arising out of strikes should it so happen.

Political action must be stimulated, and the Trade Unionists in particular and the workers in general must be educated to the power they have still left in their own hands, in spite of the adverse decision of the Lords.

Apathy

The decision has, no doubt, caused great surprise, and to many some alarm. It was no surprise to me: I expected it. Neither am I so much alarmed as many of my friends. My alarm is caused more by the indifference and the apathy of the workers generally, Trade Unionists included. They seem to me, during the last few years of prosperity, to be drifting, and little noticing where to. If the decision of the Lords is an eye-opener to them, and will awaken them from their slumber, then it should be welcomed. No decision of the Lords or Commons can injure the workers if they are alert and united to their own interests. There is work for all to do just now: will it be done? If not, the position will not be allowed to remain where it is, but further privileges and rights will be encroached upon, and no one will know where we may drift to.

Depression in trade, which has now set in, will encourage employers to take advantage of the position Unions are now placed in, unless the workers prove themselves alive to the situation, which I hope and believe they will. Lords have been the chief people to stir up the war fever. Another Lord has recently stirred up a political fever. Let us hope that the Lords have also caused a stir in the Trade Unions fever.

Power to Trade Unions

Counsel's Opinion

The Times, 10 August.

Mr. S. Woods, after consulting with the members of the Parliamentary Committee of the Trade Union Congress, has obtained the opinion of counsel as to the present state of the law as given in the judgment in the Taff Vale case and what is likely to be the effect of the decision on the future position of trade unions. The opinion of counsel states: "That the position of trade unions created by the judgment in the Taff Vale case is very serious; that the funds of unregistered unions will be as liable for damages as registered unions under the decisions given. It is advised that the various unions should amend their rules so as to prevent actions being taken against the unions in their collective capacity. Counsel advises that the trade unions should take up the first case where an injunction is sought to restrain persons from picketing (as this point has not been clearly defined), and that it should be taken up under the authority of the Trade Union Congress. In counsel's opinion a great advantage has been obtained under the judgment in giving power to trade unions to sue a vindictive employer who might try to break up or otherwise injure a trade union."

Trade Unionists React

The Taff Vale decision, penalizing unions for effects of strikes, aroused militant reaction and demand for political power.

The Times, 19 September.

A meeting convened by the Social-Democratic Federation was held at the Memorial Hall, Farringdon Street, last evening, for the purpose of considering the recent decisions of the House of Lords on trade unions. Mr. H. Quelch presided, and said the meeting had been called to consider what they regarded as one of the most serious crises that had overtaken the working-class movement in this country ever since there had been in trade unionism any organization whatever. It had been said that they should not take too gloomy a view of the situation; but if he understood the decisions at all they could not regard the situation too seriously, for the result was to deprive trade unionists of the one weapon on which they hitherto relied in their strikes and lock-outs. The time had now come for them to consider whether they should not revise the aim of trade unionism by seeking to destroy capitalism, rather than make terms with it, and whether, instead of organizing their unions for the purpose of gaining a penny more here or twopence there, they should not organize for the purpose of fighting capital to the finish, doing so on the basis of capturing the whole political machinery of the country, and using it for their social emancipation.

Challenge

W. C. Steadman declared that if trade unionism could not solve the labour problem there was no organization that could. He welcomed the decision of the House of Lords in the Taff Vale case because it would awaken the energies of the trade unionists, who had been resting on their oars since 1885. The most practical answer they could make to the House of Lords would be not to waste their money and energy in trying to get the law altered, but at the next general election to send 100 labour members to the House of Commons. Mr. Will Thorne said that after all their talk they must get to the bed-rock principle of sending labour members and Socialists to the House of Commons, and the organized workers would have to combine to pay them a weekly salary when they were there. Ways and means might be found later on to enable them to cheat the law, but he did not believe in their spending a lot of money at present, except in regard to political action. He moved :—" That this meeting sees in this decision but the first manifestation of a general spirit of reaction likely to guide the British governing classes in their dealing with the political, economic, and social problems, and therefore calls upon the workers to organize themselves in the unions into a definite class-conscious political party in order to obtain control of political power as a means to complete collective ownership and control of all the instruments of production as a means to the emancipation of the working class from the domination of capitalism."

The New Labour Movement

The miners were the first to start raising funds to support their own MPs in Parliament before the days of salaried MPs.

Morning Leader, 19 October.

The *Speaker* prints this morning a thoughtful article from a correspondent upon the " New Labour Movement "—that is, the decision of the Miners' Federation, which may well be followed by other trade societies, to raise £17,000 a year for political purposes. The plan is for each of the 345,000 miners who constitute the Federation to contribute one shilling per annum in order to secure and maintain representatives of their own in Parliament. The theoretical objection to the scheme is, of course, that it aims at class representation. The justification of democracy—which is a form of government, not a section of the public—is that it puts political power not in the hands of certain families (as in aristocracies) nor in the hands of wealthy men (as in oligarchies) but in the hands of the whole community. Class representation is, therefore, opposed to its very essence. But at a particular stage of development certain classes may have obtained such an undue political power that the truly democratic course is, for the time being, to redress the balance by specially seeking representation for other classes. Is not that the case to-day in England? The new movement is therefore to be welcomed. If it paves the way for State payment of members and of election expenses, so much the better.

On the Air

The theory of radio waves had been developed in 1864, but Marconi was the first man to achieve radio communication. In 1899 he successfully transmitted signals over the English Channel, and in 1901 made the first transatlantic signals.

Marconi Signals Across the Atlantic

Electrical World, 21 and 28 December.

The readers of Sunday newspapers were treated with a sensation of the first order by the announcement last Sunday morning that Marconi had received during the previous week several signals at St. Johns, Newfoundland, transmitted from Cornwall, England. It now appears that before leaving England Marconi made plans for accomplishing this result, though it was given out that his object in coming to Newfoundland was to establish a station for communication with ships at sea. It is quite probable that the publication of the results achieved was unauthorized, the experiments being merely preliminary ones of a scientific rather than practical nature.

Poldhu to Signal Hill

The distance between the Cornwall station at Poldhu, Cornwall, from which the signals were sent, and that on Signal Hill, Newfoundland, where they were received, is about-2,100 land miles. The signals consisted in repetitions of three dots, corresponding to the letter " S " in the Morse code, and were audible in a delicate telephone connected with the receiving apparatus.

Before leaving England, Marconi had arranged with the electrician in charge of the Cornwall station, to begin sending signals daily after a certain date, which Marconi would cable him upon perfecting his arrangements at St. Johns, where he arrived several weeks ago. Signal Hill, at the entrance to the harbour, was selected as an experimenting station, and his equipment was installed there. On December 9 he called the Poldhu station to begin sending signals at 3 p.m. daily, and to continue them until 6 p.m., these hours being, respectively, 11.30 a.m. to 2.30 p.m., St. Johns time. During these hours on Wednesday Marconi elevated a kite with an aerial wire. He remained at the recorder attached to the receiving apparatus, and, to his profound satisfaction, signals were received by him at intervals, according to the programme arranged previously with the operator at Poldhu.

An unexpected development following the announcement of Marconi's success was a warning from the Anglo-American Telegraph Company that if he persists in his work in Newfoundland an injunction will be served. In a letter served on Marconi on Sunday the solicitors of the cable company gave notice on behalf of the company that the sole and exclusive rights to operate or construct any system or means by which telegraphic communication is obtained from any places in the colony or within the jurisdiction of the government of the colony to places outside the colony are owned by it.

Atmospherics

One point which is of great value and interest to the scientific world is that Marconi has proved conclusively that the curvature of the earth is no obstacle to the system of wireless telegraphy. Some were inclined to think, and there were many heated discussions upon it, that the curvature limited the system.

All Marconi's efforts of late have been directed toward perfecting and making his sending apparatus more powerful and giving a greater height to the sending end. It still remains to be proved, however, that heavy banks of fog, low hanging clouds and heavy showers along and in the path of the transmitted electric wave will not entirely obstruct its progress. The presumption generally is that they will, as experiments thus far have proved them so. Atmospheric conditions have also much to do with and strongly affect the electric wave.

One great drawback of the system is that you cannot work more than one set of instruments at any one time between any two continents on account of mutual interference. Marconi deserves great credit for pushing this great work so persistently and intelligently, and it is only to be regretted that there are so many so-called scientists and electricians who are trying to get around Marconi's patent and thus deprive him and his people of the credit and benefits of the work to which they are fully entitled.

Costs of Communication

Marconi's achievement in first detecting a wireless telegraphic signal from across the Atlantic naturally draws attention to the spot on which the feat was accomplished. This is not the first time that the island of Newfoundland has formed a centre of interest from such a cause, for it was there, in 1858, that the earliest word came in over the transatlantic cable. The condition of distance ruled it thus in the one case as in the other, for this triangular island forms virtually the elbow of the continent, stretching out farthest of any point in the temperate zone toward the European shore.

Mr. Marconi referred to the important factor in the progress of civilization which lies in a facility of communication between different countries and said further:

" If my system of wireless telegraphy can be commercially established between different parts of the earth, of the possibility of which I may state, I have not the slightest doubt, it would bring about an enormous cheapening in the methods of communication at present existing. The system of submarine cables of to-day fulfils the demands of communication to a great extent. But the great cost of the cables themselves and their heavy working expenses cause the existing method to be beyond the reach of a majority of the people inhabiting the various countries of the world. But could this new method be applied, I believe the cost of what we now call cabling to England might be reduced at least twentyfold. The present rates are 25 cents a word. I do not see why, eventually, with the wireless system, this cost should not be reduced to one cent a word or less."

Marconi Company

Marconi and the primitive receivers in Newfoundland which made radio history.

Marconi Company

Raising the kite which hoisted Marconi's aerial on Signal Hill, Newfoundland.

The Telegraphone

Nature, 20 June

Herr Poulsen's invention fully deserves to be called one of the most astonishing that have been made of late years. That the delicate vibrations of the human voice could be changed into variations of an electric current and thus be transmitted over a distance and reproduced at the far end came as a surprise to men of science a quarter of a century ago. With no less surprise do we learn to-day that these telephonic currents, small though they are, can yet be used to create permanent magnetic fields in a steel wire, which will thus be made to serve as a tablet on which to write one's speech. It is not to be wondered at that when Herr Poulsen's discovery was announced many were incredulous as to its genuineness; the invention is precisely of the kind that one does not believe could be practical until one has actually seen or heard it in operation. That it will have the effect of putting the phonograph on an entirely new basis no one who has heard it can doubt. The speech reproduced by the telegraphone is almost as much superior to that reproduced by the wax cylinder phonograph as are the living pictures of the kinematograph to those of the zoetrope. There is none of the very unpleasant twang inseparable from the ordinary phonograph; the speech is as clear and distinct as that transmitted through a good telephone.

The Telautograph

Nature, 20 June.

The problem of devising an apparatus which should telegraphically transmit the actual handwriting or drawing of the person sending the message is one which has attracted a number of inventors. The difficulties to be overcome are, however, numerous, and in consequence up to the present no really satisfactory instrument has been invented. These difficulties seem to have been mastered in Mr. Ritchie's telautograph in a very ingenious manner, and the instrument is one which should prove thoroughly trustworthy and serviceable.

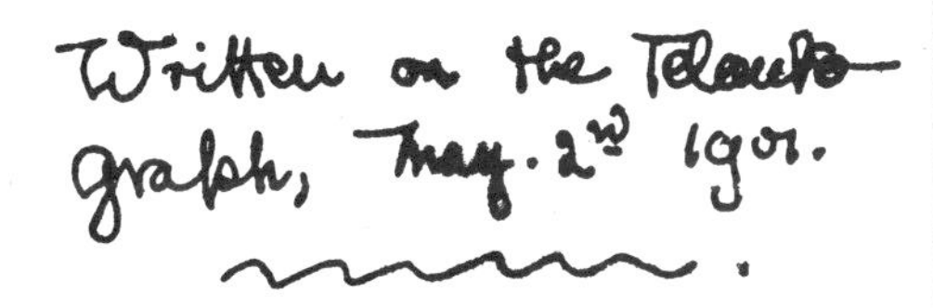

EXTRA-TERRESTRIAL COMMUNICATION

Messages from Mars

The Star, 3 January

To the Editor.

Sir, With regard to the interesting speculations lately indulged in by scientists on the subject of the planet Mars, and the supposed signals being made by the Martians to attract our attention here, it may be worth while to note the observations of that distinguished Frenchman, M. Flammarion. This able student of nature does not quite agree with those who are absolutely convinced of the genuineness of the "messages from Mars," and he accounts for the recent curious "flashing of chemical fires" from Mars by the suggestion that these were produced by the effect of the setting sun upon the Mars atmosphere. M. Flammarion's opinions or theories naturally call for the highest respect, but as we have been keeping a sharp eye on our neighbouring planet for so long, would not this sight of the effect of the setting sun have become more or less familiar by now? M. Flammarion does well to be cautious and sceptical, but this view does not appear to have occurred to him.

He further says that the possibility of Mars being inhabited by a human race more intelligent than our own is a natural conclusion of the observations which he and others have made. Does M. Flammarion believe, after all his researches, that the human class of animal on this planet has reached his present stage of pre-eminence by other means than those of chance, or what may be called "good luck," in the development of species? Broadminded men who have made any study of the origin and development of the various forms of animal life on the earth would hardly feel justified in taking the arrogant view that man got ahead of the other species by superior intellectual powers. Intellectually now, of course, he is superior to all other animals, but has not his position in this respect been produced as a process of education? If the dog or the horse had got ahead of him in the early ages in the use of his feet or paws, would he not have learnt to talk, make books, and all the rest?

Why should we assume that the development of animal life on Mars has gone on upon exactly similar lines to those which obtained upon this disordered and insignificant planet? We may find out in time, when we do get into communicative touch with Mars, that the leading animal there is a horse, and that what we call the human species occupies but a subservient position. Society lady horses there may be leading well-bred men about the parks as pets, and writing to the "Earth" or the "Star," or whatever happens to be the leading paper, complaining about the muzzling order! The horse may be practising at the Bar in Mars, stockbroking, editing the newspapers. The lot of man there may be to haul rickshaws or carts about the streets, driven by ponies or

young colts, who smoke " fags " while they distribute their bundles of special " Stars " or early " Earths." Man, for all we know, may have to eat his dinner out of a nosebag while the colt goes into some public-house for a peck of oats and a bucket of shandygaff! Who knows? Not the gifted M. Flammarion nor any other of the poor groping creatures of this planet, who, having got ahead of the other creatures, have the presumption to assume that their physical form is identical with that of the Creator of all things.—Yours, &c.,
Sundowner.
London, 1 Jan.

Epoch-making

Star, 3 January.

Mr. Nikola Tesla, the well-known electrician, who is at Chicago, sent a strangely-worded new century greeting to one of the large watch-night meetings. It ran: " I have observed electrical actions which have given me the deep conviction that before long human beings on this earth will turn their eyes to the firmament above with feelings of love and reverence, thrilled by glad news. Brethren, we have a message from another world, unknown and remote. It reads: ' One, two, three.' "

[Human imagination is a strictly limited quantity, and if " Sundowner " desires another illustration of the inability of even ingenious minds to " imagine " anything outside their mundane experience he should turn to Mr. Wells's " War of the Worlds." It is a thrilling story, but when Mr. Wells tries to realise a Martian for us he becomes fantastically feeble.—Ed.]

Mother Earth's Leading-strings

H. G. Wells's " feeble " imagination (see Star *Editor's note above) continued to intrigue his readers for at least another seventy years. Here, Wells's first astronauts land on the moon: an extract from his novel* The First Men in the Moon (1901).

He sat down on the edge of the manhole, he let his feet drop until they were within six inches of the lunar ground. He hesitated for a moment, then thrust himself forward, dropped these intervening inches, and stood upon the untrodden soil of the moon.

As he stepped forward he was refracted grotesquely by the edge of the glass. He stood for a moment looking this way and that. Then he drew himself together and leapt.

The glass distorted everything, but it seemed to me even then to be an extremely big leap. He had at one bound become remote. He seemed twenty or thirty feet off. He was standing high upon a rocky mass and gesticulating back to me. Perhaps he was shouting—but the sound did not reach me. But how the deuce had he done this? I felt like a man who has just seen a new conjuring trick.

In a puzzled state of mind I too dropped through the manhole. I stood up. Just in front of me the snowdrift had fallen away and made a sort of ditch. I made a step and jumped.

I found myself flying through the air, saw the rock on which he stood coming to meet me, clutched it and clung in a state of infinite amazement.

I gasped a painful laugh. I was tremendously confused. Cavor bent down and shouted in piping tones for me to be careful.

I had forgotten that on the moon, with only an eighth part of the earth's mass and a quarter of its diameter, my weight was barely a sixth what it was on earth. But now that fact insisted on being remembered.

" We are out of Mother Earth's leading-strings now," he said.

The Open Road

The manufacture of petrol-driven cars began in 1885. Though American demand was high, in Britain cars were legally controlled as " light locomotives " (needing a man to walk in front with a red flag) which retarded development for a decade.

Record Broken.

New York Tribune, headline, 17 November.

Fournier speeds his automobile a mile in 51.45 seconds on Ocean Parkway, Brooklyn.

Omnibuses

From Improved Means of Locomotion as a first step towards, the Cure of Housing Difficulties of London, *by Charles Booth.*

They certainly have their uses, but that they should up to now form the principal method of transit on so many of our main routes is evidence of how far London has fallen behind in the adoption of methods which other cities have long regarded as essential.

Traffic congestion, 1901-style.

Guildhall

Race is Off

The £1,000 Motor Contest to Take Place in Paris

Morning Leader, 7 December.

The big projected motor-car race between London and Brighton, which was to have taken place to-day, has been ruled " off "—but only for the time being.

The opponents, Mr. J. V. F. Scudder, of Boston, and Mr. Dick Farman, the head of the big Automobile agency in Long-acre, are determined to settle the relative merits of their respective cars, and their future plans were confided to a " Morning Leader " representative yesterday by Mr. Farman.

The race, it will be remembered, was to have been over 110 miles of road, for a prize of £1,000. The opposition came from the Automobile Club, and the intimation was conveyed that such a race would be run in open defiance of the law, and that those who participated in such contests acted as enemies to the motor movement.

" We received the message," said Mr. Farman comically, " at about nine o'clock on Thursday night—but the whole affair," and Mr. Farman shrugged his shoulders, " was really very hastily conceived. We were driving home from a private dinner on Wednesday evening, and I suppose we got talking about the superior qualities of our machines, and then—well, it led to a challenge. It is annoying," added Mr. Farman, " that it came out at all; it had no business to."

It so happens, and perhaps fortunately, that both Mr. Farman and Mr. Scudder are members of the Automobile Club. Mr. Farman has spent practically the whole of his life in Paris, and enjoyed the recent satisfaction of gaining fifth place in the Paris-Berlin race.

" There was a statement," said Mr. Farman quietly, " about our having mutually consented to slow down to 16 miles an hour! whilst passing through villages and towns. Might I be allowed to remark that it was six ? Thank you."

After a few remarks about the morals of motor-racing in England, Mr. Farman said that the race would be run in Paris—sometime this month, though the actual date had not yet been fixed upon; and the course would be between Paris and Melun and back.

"The real interest in the race," concluded Mr. Farman, "is the proof whether a light car is superior to a heavy one, or vice versa. Mr. Scudder rides a Daimler, weighing roughly 1 ton and $\frac{1}{8}$, and with 14 nominal h.p., and my car is a Morisse, weighing 1,200lb., with 10 nominal h.p. In the face of the big Paris-Vienna race next year, when all cars weighing over 2,000lb. will be debarred, the result should be of particular interest."

Automobilists United

The Times, 2 March.

It was decided to form a "Motor union under the auspices of the Automobile Club"; open to all motorists, ladies or gentlemen, without reference to social position, by which all automobilists shall be embodied under one banner for the purpose of furthering the motor movement.

BROTHERS IN ADVERSITY.

Farmer. "PULL UP, YOU FOOL! THE MARE'S BOLTING!"
Motorist. "SO'S THE CAR!"

Punch/Mary Evans Picture Library

Military Autocars

Favourable Report from the Recent German Manoeuvres

Daily Chronicle, 4 January 1902.

Automobiles have secured their place as part of the equipment of the German army.

Reporting on the trials of various types of the new methods of locomotion during the recent manoeuvres the "Militär Wochenblatt" acknowledges that it must be employed in the next war. The organ of the German army authorities continues:

"To the 17th Army Corps were attached two Fowler road-locomotives of the Malta type, capable of drawing three loaded ordinary waggons. In spite of the accumulation of mud and the presence of deep puddles, these entirely fulfilled their purpose along the roads, and also successfully accomplished short distances across the open country.

"Difficulties arose when waggons loaded with bivouacking necessaries had to be transported across land rendered spongy by the constant rain. In these cases the road-locomotives fulfilled their object by remaining stationary from time to time, and then drawing the waggons up to them by means of a wire rope.

"At all events, the recent manoeuvres represent a decided step forward towards the general employment of automobiles in our army."

The Horseless Carriage

Motor Car Journal, 6 July.

At Cardiff, George Thornton was summoned for driving a motor-car "at a greater speed than reasonable". The Stipendiary, accepting the evidence of the police that the car was propelled at a rate of 10 miles an hour, which he held with great confidence to be ... an unreasonable and ... dangerous speed, imposed a fine of £5.

Furiously Driving

Motor Car Journal, 2 November.

At Croydon, Edgar Cundy, of South Norwood, was summoned for furiously driving a motor-car in Brighton Road, South Croydon, on October 13th. The police evidence as to speed was conflicting, various estimates ranging from 16 to 153 m.p.h.

Threat from the Sea

Eighteenth-century attempts at submarines were unsuccessful. But in 1875 an American design proved viable, and was adopted by the British navy. In the 1914-18 war, submarines were to play a vital part.

The First British Submarine

The Illustrated London News, 12 October.

The first of the five submarines of the *Holland* type which are being prepared for his Majesty's Navy was launched on Oct. 2 at Barrow Yard. The launch was as unusual as the craft itself, for there was no ceremony, and the vessel left the ways unnamed and unnumbered. The boat is so constructed as to offer the least possible resistance to the water when cruising on the surface, where her motive power will be a gasoline engine with a maximum speed of about nine knots an hour. When the vessel is submerged, she will be propelled by an electrical motor at a speed of seven knots an hour for a four hours' run. The current will be supplied from storage batteries, and the vessel will be lighted by incandescent electric lamps. There is provision for storage of compressed air for ventilation, and the steering and diving are to be regulated by hand. The submarine measures 63 ft.

The German Navy

The German navy was fast becoming a challenge to Britain's hitherto unique sea-power.

The Times, 2 March.

The Budget Committee of the Reichstag continued the discussion of the navy estimates to-day. A resolution was carried by a large majority requesting the Imperial Chancellor to consider in the interests of economy the advisability of establishing Government works for the manufacture of armour plates. In reply to a question Admiral von Tirpitz said that he had not been able to modify his unfavourable opinion of submarine vessels. In spite of attempts which had been made to improve these boats it was still impossible to make any use of them. The German navy would keep the matter in view, but there was for the present no occasion to make experiments of their own.

The first submarine for service in the Royal Navy was launched in October 1901 at Barrow. Ironically, the design had been made by an Irish-American hoping for the destruction of the British navy.

Taking off

Gliders and balloons apart, flight had yet to be achieved. Though experiments were numerous at this time (the invention of the petrol engine was a turning-point), it was not until 1903 that the Wright brothers were to achieve powered flight.

Balloon Ascent

Exciting Incidents at the Crystal Palace Yesterday.

Morning Leader, 7 December.

A balloon ascent—the second of a series—was made under the auspices of the recently-formed Aero Club from the grounds of the Crystal Palace yesterday afternoon, the passengers in the balloon, which was furnished by Messrs. Spencer, being Mr. C. Pollock, a well-known ballooning amateur, and the Hon. C. F. Rolls, the automobilist.

On account of a brisk and varying wind considerable difficulty attended the start, which was made at about midday. During the process of taking in ballast the aeronauts were placed in a position of some risk owing to the erratic movements of the balloon, which, notwithstanding the efforts of 14 or 15 assistants, was frequently lifted to a considerable height and again depressed by alternating puffs of wind, the car at each descent striking the ground with great violence, so much that the two passengers were obliged to exercise all their agility to save themselves from being precipitated from the car.

As it was, a valuable aneroid barometer, used for measuring altitude, was detached from its fastenings and thrown to the ground, being hopelessly damaged by the concussion.

An element of an amusing nature was introduced into the incident by the preparations for photographing the balloon and its occupants. It was utterly impossible to keep the vessel at rest, and under these circumstances it was allowed to ascend about 20ft., in which situation two photographs were successfully taken; while a third picture was being attempted the wind again lifted the balloon sharply, and the men who were holding the vessel down were carried off their feet directly, a wild scramble immediately resulting. Ultimately an excellent ascent was made, the balloon disappearing in a south-easterly direction.

The descent was made on the banks of the Thames near Gravesend. Soon after the ascent the wind was due west, but it veered towards the south, and the aeronauts were forced to bring the voyage to a hasty conclusion in order to prevent their being carried out to sea.

What is an Aeroplane?

From the first issue of Flying, *25 November.*

The essential features of a practicable, safe, and useful aerial vehicle, are:

1. The ability to raise itself and freight, either from a level track after a short initial run (being on wheels) or by gravity after running down a gentle slope or inclined staging near the ground.
2. The ability to propel itself in any desired direction, and be practically unobstructed by an average wind.
3. To offer comparatively small obstructive surface to the air or to the wind.
4. To be so constructed and poised, and to have such stability, that it cannot capsize nor fall precipitately.
5. The generator furnace (in steam) to be so enclosed and under control, as regards both fuel and air supply, that the fire can be regulated to a nicety or instantly extinguished.
6. Lastly, the machine should be comparable with the fastest land vehicles. It is not expected that a hundred miles or more per hour will be maintained. The gain will be mainly in going by the shortest cut to any desired place.

Vanity Fair

Alberto Santos Dumont, one of the most intrepid balloonists of his age, in " Santos Dumont 5 ".

Railways for New Markets

The spread of railway-building affected the course of history in many ways, bringing scattered colonies into contact, enabling workers to commute to factories distant from their homes, and opening up resources in hitherto inaccessible interiors. Of the £2,000 million Britain had invested in other countries (half of them in the Empire) much went into the building of railways which, coupled with Britain's readiness to import goods and to export coal, helped world trade to expand.

The Uganda Railroad

Railroad Gazette (U.S.A.), 27 December.

The Uganda Railroad is at last completed, at least so far completed that on December 20 a locomotive reached Lake Victoria Nyanza at Port Florence, the lake terminus of the road. This sounds almost like a miracle. It is hard to realize that a railroad had actually been built from deep water to the equatorial lakes, bringing Usogo, Uganda and Unyoro within a few hours of the British commercial and naval fleets. So far as concerns the betterment of condition of Equatorial Africa nothing more important has ever been done. We are not speaking now of the Soudan, a semi-civilized Mohammedan country, but of Equatorial Africa, a savage country of pagan negroes.

The people of Continental Europe have taken fresh alarm and look upon this as the British conquest of Africa. So it is, but it is a matter of vastly more importance to the negroes of Africa and to the broad interests of humanity than to the people of the British Islands. No man of information supposes that the railroad will pay materially more than working expenses. It will do well to do that. The interest charges will be lost for a generation or two; but this is the only sound way to attack savage Central Africa, if any one thinks that he ought to attack it. It is at least rational while the Cape-to-Cairo project is irrational. But we cannot now take time to develop this fascinating topic.

We have chronicled the progress of the Uganda Railroad from the time of Major Macdonald's reconnaissance and report in 1891, and we shall recapitulate now only a few facts. The railroad is from Mombasa, on the Indian Ocean, to the northeastern corner of the Victoria Lake. Its ocean end is at latitude four, south, and its lake end is a few minutes south of the equator. The line as built is said by the press despatches to be 582 miles long. This is probably not far out of the way, and perhaps is exact. Major Macdonald's estimate was 657 miles. The latest report that we have here is that of Sir Guilford Molesworth, when the surveys were still not completed and the length of line could only be roughly approximated. Some parts of the line are over a very difficult profile, the highest summit being about 7,500 ft. above the sea. We believe that the ruling grade on the steepest slope is a little more that 100 ft. to the mile.

The original notion that cheap native labor could be used broke down, and the workmen had to be brought from India; this fact, together with great mortality, the destruction of animals by the tsetse fly, the unexpectedly difficult country and the entire lack of natural resources, such as timber and coal, must have made the line really very costly for a light, narrow gage road. (It is meter gage.) The original estimate, made on the report of Major Macdonald was £3,422 per mile; but when the rail-head had reached the 225th mile the cost had run up nearly £5,000 per mile, and the worst of the job had not been reached. Sir Guilford Molesworth thought it not improbable that the cost would be at least £7,000 per mile, but he estimated that a considerable part of the charge on the capital invested would be saved indirectly by the reduced cost of patrolling the Indian Ocean for the suppression of slavery.

The British Uganda Railroad is not only built by coolies from Hindoostan, but it is worked by a staff of Indian employees, who have mostly received their training on the Indian railroads. They are probably the only tropical people capable of supplying a great force of locomotive engineers, telegraphers, station agents, etc. They are not proof against the African coast climate, however. At times as many as 70 per cent. of the coolies employed in construction have been disabled by malaria. The coolies live in villages along the line, and these villages are surrounded by palisades to keep out the lions, which are numerous and have killed many men. The coolies are paid about five dollars a month.

Pax Britannica, by Rail

The Times, 21 December

A telegram from Mombasa announces that the laying of the rails of the Uganda Railway has been completed, the railhead having reached the shore of Lake Victoria Nyanza on Thursday last. Platelaying began on August 5, 1896, and thus within less than five years and a half of its inception this great and arduous undertaking has been brought to a successful conclusion. The railway is altogether 572 miles long, but its mere length conveys no idea of the difficulties which had to be overcome in carrying the steel track up from the shores of the Indian Ocean to the great plateau of the Central African lakes, more than 3,000 feet above the level of the sea, over intervening ranges of twice that altitude and more. The road had frequently to be cut through dense forests or hewn out of the rock, bridges had to be built over streams subject to the sudden rise and fall of tropical rains, in the lowlands malarial fever of a virulent type had to be reckoned with, and the attacks to which working parties were often exposed in the jungle from wild beasts disturbed for the first time in their hereditary lairs added a new and serious danger, certainly unprecedented on such a scale, to the task of railway construction.

The Cost

The cost has been proportionately great. Up to the end of the last financial year the expenditure incurred amounted to £4,115,002, or, including the estimates for the current year, to £4,815,002. Yet there are few people in this country who would now question the great utility of this expenditure, though it may be interesting to remember how lukewarm was the support it received from the then Chancellor of the Exchequer, Sir William Harcourt, and other Liberals of his complexion when the first vote was passed by the House of Commons in 1895, just before the last Liberal Administration went out of office. Then, as now, the school of Radical politicians whom Lord Rosebery so aptly described the other night as " sitting still with the fly-blown phylacteries bound round their obsolete policy," were loth to recognize either the responsibilities which a great Imperial position involves, or the statesmanship which demands present sacrifices to assure the future development of a great Imperial inheritance.

Sir Harry Johnston, in the exhaustive report which he addressed to the Foreign Office on his return this year from Uganda, has supplied material evidence that the Uganda Protectorate will, as he says, not only justify and redeem in the future the money expended on its creation and development, but will further console us for similar expenditure on the less richly-endowed Protectorate of East Africa. Nor is it a small thing, though Sir William Harcourt scarcely concealed his contempt for this aspect of the question at the time, that the *Pax Britannica* has secured order and security over a vast region richly endowed by nature with a population of nearly 4,000,000 souls, which until the advent of British rule was given over to a cruel and sterilizing tyranny.

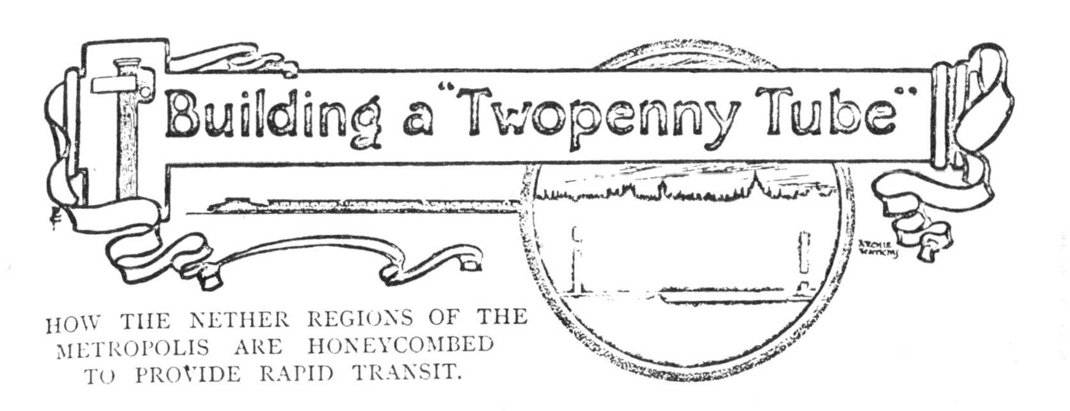

HOW THE NETHER REGIONS OF THE METROPOLIS ARE HONEYCOMBED TO PROVIDE RAPID TRANSIT.

The world's first underground railway had been built in London in 1863, four miles long. It was the brain-child of a solicitor, and conceived as the answer to traffic congestion. The network was much increased around 1901, and today is nearly 100 miles long.

London Magazine.

One of the most perplexing problems that confronts the civic authorities of many of the great cities of the world to-day is the possible means of relieving the streets of the congested traffic, so as to ensure more rapid transit from one point to another. And probably this question is of more vital importance in the case of London than any other city on the globe. As aerial navigation is not yet an accomplished fact, the only alternative left to us is to burrow through the earth like rabbits, and thus by subterranean railways accelerate our means of travelling. In this respect London has set the example to the rest of the world, and the experiment has been attended with such conspicuous success that in a short space of time the metropolis will be undermined by an immense web of " tubes."

One of the latest of these projected railways is that running from Baker Street in the West End, to Waterloo on the south side of the river Thames. When completed it will tap some of the busiest and most fashionable hives of business in the metropolis, and can afford communication between some of the great trunk lines to the north and south of the country respectively.

At the present moment some £50,000,000 capital is invested in these contemplated enterprises. The time is not far remote when London will be better supplied with means of locomotion than any other city in the world. The Government has realised that the " tubes " offer the only practical solution to the crucial problem of relieving the thoroughfares of their congested traffic, and are encouraging their construction accordingly.

Life and Labour

With nearly 80 per cent of the population now in towns, the conscience of the nation was beginning to be stirred by the conditions of the urban poor when Rowntree (a young Quaker businessman, later to become chairman of the family chocolate firm) produced his factual report on conditions in York. The average wages at this time were stagnant, at 18s.—21s. for a 54-hour week. The poorest boys were 3½ inches shorter and 11 lb. lighter than the rest. Poverty was a main reason why one in three volunteers for the Boer War (at a shilling a day) were rejected as medically unfit, even though the Army accepted recruits only 5 feet tall.

Family Life

Rowntree, on Poverty.

A family living upon the scale allowed for in this estimate* must never spend a penny on railway fare or omnibus. They must never go into the country unless they walk. They must never purchase a half-penny newspaper or spend a penny to buy a ticket for a popular concert. They must write no letters to absent children, for they cannot afford to pay the postage. They must never contribute anything to their church or chapel, or give any help to a neighbour which costs them money. They cannot save, nor can they join a sick club or Trade Union, because they cannot pay the necessary subscriptions. The children must have no pocket money for dolls, marbles or sweets. The father must smoke no tobacco and must drink no beer. The mother must never buy any pretty clothes for herself or for her children, the character of the family wardrobe as for the family diet being governed by the regulation, "Nothing must be bought but that which is absolutely necessary for the maintenance of physical health, and what must be bought must be of the plainest description." Should a child fall ill, it must be attended by the parish doctor: should it die, it must be buried by the parish. Finally, the wage earner must never be absent from his work for a single day.

** A minimum wage, 21s. 8d., for the support of a couple with three children.*

RTHPL

Bare feet and rags: commonplace sights in London slums at the turn of the century.

A Review of Rowntree's Book on Poverty

The Times, 21 December.

Mr. B. Seebohm Rowntree's book on *Poverty* supplements Mr. Charles Booth's collective inquiry into the life and labour of the people in London by a similar study carried out in a typical provincial town. Working on a smaller scale Mr. Rowntree has been able to make a more minute investigation, and has produced an instructive record of observations on the actual conditions of life among the "working-class" population of York. York is a town of medium size and average character. The

RTHPL

RTHPL

population is 77,793, according to the census of 1901, but at the time of Mr. Rowntree's investigation it was reckoned at about 76,000. He divides it into seven classes as follows:—(*a*) Family income under 18s. a week, 2.6 per cent.; (*b*) 18s. and under 21s., 5.9 per cent.; (*c*) 21s. and under 30s., 20.7 per cent.; (*d*) over 30s., 32.4 per cent. The three remaining classes are domestic servants, servant-keeping households, and persons in public institutions. The first four classes represent the "wage-earning" families of York; they number 11,560 households and 46,754 persons. The book embodies the results of a house-to-house visitation of these 11,560 families. The average weekly earnings from all sources, including children and lodgers, were found to be 32s. 8¾d. per family. This points to a pretty high standard of prosperity, considering that house rent is low in York, and the average size of families only 4.04 persons; if the income were evenly distributed there would be no real poverty at all. That, of course, is not the case; families are large and small, profitable and expensive; wages are good and bad; there is sickness and health. Nevertheless, Mr. Rowntree's estimate that 43.4 per cent. of the wage-earning classes—equivalent to nearly one-third of the whole population—are actually living in poverty is surprising. The statement, as it stands, seems hardly reconcilable with the average income and the classification of population given above; it would certainly be misleading without explanation.

It has been reached by laying down a special definition of poverty, to which some exception may be taken. The criterion adopted is the expenditure on food required for a standard diet, which contains so much "protein" and will produce so many "calories." In other words, poverty is reduced to a chemical formula. Mr. Rowntree evidently has a robust faith in physiological chemistry, which is hardly justified by the elementary state of that science, and no less confidence in the "average" man and his "standard" requirements. But life is not governed by formulae, and the attempt to measure appetites leads the reformer into a quandary, for it will be found—and is found in this book—that everybody takes either too little or too much. Both are bad for health and it is hard to say which is worse, to be ill from over-eating or inefficient from under-eating. In the next place Mr. Rowntree's poor consist of two classes, "primary" and "secondary." The former are families whose total earnings are insufficient to purchase the standard of diet in addition to other necessaries. They number 1,465 households and 7,230 persons, being nearly 10 per cent. of the population. The "secondary" poor are families whose earnings are not insufficient but are not applied to that purpose. This class is nearly twice as large as the "primary." Now it is certain that in a large proportion of cases some of the earnings which might, but do not, go to buy necessaries are wilfully thrown away. Mr. Rowntree refers to the prevalence of betting in York. It is, in truth, a great field for the bookmaker, who probably absorbs nearly as much of the working man's money as the publican. As for the latter, publichouses are said to be much in excess of the requirements—1 to 330 persons—but they are evidently not sufficient for the appetite of the people, who have supplemented them by nine purely "drinking" clubs, in addition to five "political" ones where drink is sold. In one of these clubs members often remain all night, and even from Saturday to Monday; at another the bill for intoxicants in 1899 was £1,612. But the word poverty in its ordinary sense is not properly applied to persons who might live in comfort if they did not squander money on betting and drink. For these reasons Mr. Rowntree's book is not altogether satisfactory as a statistical study. On the other hand, the detailed observations are of great interest, and particularly a series of "family budgets," which are true human "documents." There is one item that occurs in every one and would repay further investigation—namely, life insurance. The author reckons that the wage-earning classes in York pay not less than £400 a week, or 8¼d. per family, for insurance. What do they get for it? The item always appears in expenditure, but never in receipts. Does it all go in funerals with attendant festivities?

Morning Leader

New Hope

The final sentence in Rowntree's Report on Poverty.

The dark shadow of the Malthusian philosophy has passed away, and no view of the ultimate scheme of things would now be accepted under which multitudes of men and women are doomed by inevitable law to struggle for existence so severe as necessary to cripple or destroy the higher parts of their nature.

Sunday Music in the Workhouse

Good works by the charitable, treats and sacred music were highspots for the paupers and other inmates of workhouses.

Graphic, 12 January.

Every winter the National Sunday League gives concerts on Sundays at the metropolitan workhouses. This good work has now been in progress for five or six years, and the first concert of this season was given recently at the City Road Workhouse. The Sunday concert is a rare treat to the inmates. If one may form an opinion of all paupers by a visit to one workhouse, then they all love their music on Sundays. As a rule they get plenty of it—from a harmonium, and strictly sacred. The band and vocalists sent by the National Sunday League, however, have a programme in which the sacred music is—dare we say lightened?—by the addition of some national airs. One has only to go to one of these concerts to see what pleasure the old men and women derive from it.

THE CENSUS

A census has been taken in Britain every ten years since 1801 (except in 1941). It has acted as a stocktaking of the population, their ages, sex, occupations, housing and other statistics useful to national planning.

Crowded Homes Make Problems for Census Officials

Daily Telegraph, 27 March.

There are grim problems connected with the census. In the East-end of London the enumerators are brought face to face with difficulties that are unknown in Suburbia, where an indisposition on the part of ladies to reveal their ages is playfully supposed to be prevalent, and in Flatland, where the curiosity of the hall porter or liftman and the inquisitiveness of one's neighbours are imagined to be incurable. In Whitechapel, probably the most congested district in the whole of the metropolis, the numbering of the people is rendered no light task, first, because of the large increase in the number of aliens; next, on account of the overcrowding to which their presence has led; and thirdly, by reason of the flotsam and jetsam character of the British-born population. Whitechapel, however, is fortunate in having as superintendent-registrar a gentleman of unique experience. The present is the seventh census in which he has taken part, for Mr. Vallance was a youth in the office of the superintendent when the census of 1851 was made, in 1861 was assistant-registrar, and as superintendent-registrar has since had to prepare the returns each decade—1871, 1881, 1891, and 1901, his seventh census having been the London quinquennial in 1896. With a thorough knowledge of the locality and the remarkable changes that have come about, Mr. Vallance is in the hopes of furnishing to the Registrar-General a complete return, which may be expected to throw considerable light upon the present social condition of a quarter of London that has earned, in spite of itself, an unenviable notoriety.

Destitute

In Whitechapel is comprised also Spitalfields, Mile-end New Town, Aldgate, the Tower, Old Artillery Ground, and Norton Folgate—an area of 460 acres, with an estimated population of 80,000. It is not necessary to go back more than a quarter of a century to recall the old Black Horse—the highwayman's house of call—in its declining days; or the state of the alleys opening from the high road, close to where the present Art Gallery stands, at the corner of which passages policemen were wont to warn strangers from entering, and in one of which, in a fetid hovel, the present writer saw a whole family destitute of the barest vestige of clothing. Great clearances have been made, huge model dwellings have been erected, plague-spots have been eliminated, but, nevertheless, to-day in Spitalfields 330 persons are computed to dwell upon every acre, and in Whitechapel 195. The census will show whether these estimates are correct or below the mark. In the midst of all this congestion, the appointed enumerators are now leaving the blue schedules, and are entering all sorts of homes, the character of which can best be guessed from the vivid descriptions of the Rev. W. H. Davies, who declares:

> From one of my parochial buildings I have seen through the thinly-veiled window of a house four men and six women retiring for the night in one room, the rent of which is 8s. a week—all of them respectable, hard-working people, and the majority of them sleeping in beds upon the floor.

Who would be the head of the household to fill in the schedule in such a case? There will be many of the kind, for the same local clergyman says:

> I have had a census taken of one or two typical alleys and houses in my parish. In one alley there are ten houses—51 rooms—nearly all about 8ft by 9ft—and 254 people. In six instances only do two people occupy one room, and in other rooms the numbers varied from three to nine. In another court, with six houses and twenty-two rooms, were eighty-four people, again, six, seven, eight, and nine being the number living in one room in several instances. In one house, with eight rooms, are forty-five people, one room containing nine persons, one eight, two seven, and another six. For these forty-five people there is one office, and in the case of nearly all tenement houses the washing for the family must be done by the aid of a pail, which is put upon the stove, and serves for a copper on washing days. There are practically no ovens, and such a thing as a home-made rice pudding is unknown to the children. At one of our Christmas teas, about 200 poor children were assembled. After tea, as they sat together, I asked: " How many of you live in a one-roomed home? " Every hand but seven went up. " How many live in a two-roomed home? " Seven hands went up. " How many live in three rooms? " None. " How many of you live in a ' furnished room '? " All but twelve. So that, with the exception of those twelve children, all the rest were practically homeless, the wretched contents of a " furnished room " not being the property of the tenant, and the rent of 1s. a day or more being paid, in the majority of cases, daily.

There is a little black-edged space in the left-hand corner of the schedule, with the note: " If the above persons occupy less than five rooms write in this space the number of rooms occupied by them." In Spitalfields this particular corner of the official form will be in great request.

And it is not merely in the buildings which years ago were occupied by the Spitalfields weavers and the tenements that have not disappeared with the wholesale clearances of condemned areas that overcrowding exists. In the huge " models," where the caretaker will act as the enumerator, the existence of a practice of sub-letting rooms is more than suspected. How far the census will disclose its extent remains to be seen. It is the pressure of the foreign immigrant and of the poor provincial that is answerable for much of the congestion. Many of the former class are content to pay exorbitant rent, and, having secured rooms, they intend to live under forbidden conditions, taking in lodgers so as to be rent-free. Ten years ago the number of Russians and Poles in Whitechapel was 13,000, and they have since largely increased.

" These aliens," said Mr. Vallance, " have suffered so much oppression in their own countries that they are suspicious in regard to returns; but in the present census we have the co-operation of the Jewish community, and the district has been mapped out into sections, a Jewish lady or gentleman, with helpers, taking charge of each section. Notices have been issued in Yiddish, and the Jewish clergy in the synagogues have explained to their congregations the meaning of the census. So we think that the foreign population is fairly well satisfied that there is nothing underlying it. Many of the aliens do not speak English, and the assistance of the enumerators in filling up returns for them will be necessary. Even as regards the English people it is my experience that, make a schedule as simple as you can, they do not understand the tabular form, and the enumerators will have to complete the filling-up. No, I don't anticipate difficulty in subdividing the classifications of employments, for in our ordinary register of births and deaths the trade has to be very particularly described—thus, if a man is a carpenter he must be put down as a carpenter journeyman or a carpenter foreman. The aliens will mostly represent the trades which they themselves have introduced into the district—slipper-making, boot-finishing, and cheap tailoring."

In the East-end of London, with a floating population, the enumerators will have curious experiences. The deputy of the common lodging-house, which is regarded officially as an " institution," will have to make his return as complete as he can from the details that he can extract from his lodgers, many of whom in Spitalfields are casual labourers, dock workers, market porters, and hawkers of penny novelties in the City. The common lodging-house offers a sure retreat to many a married man escaping family responsibilities, but such a refugee will scarcely volunteer his antecedents or give particulars leading to identification. And what will be the task of the enumerator in a family like this? It is an instance given recently at a conference on the subject of overcrowding. The Rev. W. H. Davies said:

I know two rooms where a poor family lives. The earnings of the man are small. The rent is high. At ten o'clock at night the family retire from the kitchen to the bed-room, and a gentlemanly-looking man with frock coat and silk hat enters the vacated kitchen and makes his bed on the floor. He helps pay the rent.

It will be the duty of the police to make a return of the " elusive " classes—the homeless and bedless, who even at this season of the year pass the night in the streets, to be " moved on," if discovered, by the constable on the beat. On Sunday night, the public-houses closing at eleven p.m., there will be less temptation to remain drinking the " lodging money " away—the spending of which generally accounts for the presence of penniless and homeless wayfarers in the byways and nooks and crannies of the great city, in spite of the multiplication of shelters and havens for this very class. And it needs an intimate knowledge of the neighbourhood to chance upon certain of the lurking places of these wanderers. In many streets where the houses are occupied by tenement lodgers, each room may be securely bolted or barred from within, but the street door is never fastened throughout the year, and the staircases and landings harbour many poor wretches in the biting hours of dawn, out of reach of police surveillance, and, it may be, beyond the view of the census enumerator.

In London's West End, often households comprised as many servants as members of the family.

Graphic

Education for the new Century

The Government Education Bill

In 1902, the Bill became an Act, authorizing county councils to pay for and supervise standards in all schools, including the voluntary ones, in their area.

Graphic, 8 June.

The Education Bill which Sir John Gorst introduced into the House of Commons a few weeks ago has so far met with little criticism except from the out-and-out supporters of School Boards. This party has convinced itself that it is impossible for the education of the people to be properly cared for except by a body chosen by popular election. What ground there is for this belief it is hard to discover. In practice the average elector knows very little about education and cares less. A few enthusiasts do, indeed, succeed in getting themselves elected to the School Boards throughout the country in spite of the dead weight of the indifference of the electors, but these are just the people who would be nominated by the County Councils to the educational committees. The truth is that the uses of popular election are more limited than the average Radical yet cares to admit.

When any great public issue is at stake it is necessary and desirable that the wishes of the people should be consulted by means of a popular election; but on the humdrum work of daily administration the average voter has no means of forming a judgment, nor is he capable of selecting men whose judgment would be of value. So far as can be foreseen Sir John Gorst's Bill, instead of diminishing public zeal for education, as the School Board party professes to believe, will very greatly increase it. The necessity for improved education is being rapidly brought home to the commercial classes in our great towns in consequence of the industrial progress made by countries that are better educated than ourselves. It is these classes who hold control upon most of the Councils in the county boroughs.

Educate for Industry

One motive in the drive for better education was the need for more skilled workers in industry (and in the army, too).

Graphic.

Now that the reign of King Edward has fairly begun, his subjects are beginning to take stock of the problems that await solution. In the region of Home politics undoubtedly the most important problem is the educational one. The country has at least been aroused to the fact that if Englishmen wish to maintain their commercial supremacy they must see that employers and employed alike are thoroughly trained for the business of their lives. We cannot safely trust any longer to good luck or to muddling through. It is the well-equipped who wins the modern race, and it is impossible to deny that some of our rivals are by their more thorough education in many respects better equipped than we are. This same problem of education, which is of supreme importance to our industrial future, is of barely less importance to our military strength.

The Cockerton Judgment

A celebrated lawsuit aroused interest in the limitations imposed on Schools' Boards, which were to provide only "elementary" education, not secondary or adult education.

The Times, 8 April

The longer the judgment in "Rex *v.* Cockerton" is looked at, the more it commends itself as resting upon an unassailable basis of common sense; and it may be hoped that the Progressive majority of the London School Board will recognize, as Sir Charles Elliott advises, the weight of the unanimous opinion of five eminent Judges, and deny themselves the luxury of further litigation at the ratepayers' expense. Stripped of legal technicalities and subtle disquisitions as to the precise meaning of certain expressions in the Education Acts, the issue was a very simple one—whether a body empowered to levy rates for the elementary education of children was justified in spending those rates either on education for children that was not elementary, as in some of their higher-grade schools, or in giving free education to adults, as in their evening continuation schools. It has for some time past been pointed out, in these columns and elsewhere, that the School Board were probably acting *ultra vires* in these respects. But appeals to the ratepayers to look after their own interests at the triennial elections, by returning candidates less pledged to progressive expenditure, have failed through the apathy of the electorate, who in one sense have largely themselves to blame if their money has been illegally expended. It was not until an auditor was found courageous and independent enough to surcharge certain items of expenditure that it was possible to test at law the validity of the practices complained of. That test has now been applied with decisive results. Even if the School Board are so ill-advised as to carry their appeal further, it is most unlikely that the House of Lords will reverse the decision that they may neither give secondary education to children nor free education to adults; and that they must confine their education within the limits of the Whitehall Code.

What is Elementary?

The appearance of the annual edition of that Code is a timely comment upon the view apparently entertained by some advocates of School Board policy, that it was necessary to overstep its limits, as well as upon the significant remarks of the Master of the Rolls as to the nature of those limits. A Code which allows in elementary schools, at the discretion of His Majesty's inspectors, such subjects as algebra, mensuration, navigation, Latin, French, and shorthand (to mention a few only of the special subjects for which grants may be given), and adds a further saving clause that "any other subject may, if sanctioned by the Board, be included in the course of instruction," can hardly be accused of drawing too low the superior limit of elementary teaching. Most people, on the contrary, will agree with Sir Archibald Smith that it already embraces the high-water mark of such education. In the face of these facts, it is absurd to talk as if the action of the auditor in this case was a blow to popular education, or as if that education in its elementary stages could not be adequately provided without recourse to the more advanced and ambitious programme of the South Kensington Directory. The Code is quite liberal enough, and the Board of Education are only doing their duty in resisting attempts to widen unduly the sphere of elementary education.

Higher-grade Board Schools

Changes introduced in this year's Code, as noted by us on Saturday, are, like most other changes in recent years, in the direction of liberality and flexibility. Nor is it any exception to this estimate that we now find incorporated in the Code itself the Minute of April, 1900, establishing "higher elementary schools" on the analogy of the French *écoles primaires supérieures.* It is over the application of this Minute and recognition of schools under it that friction has arisen between the Board of Education and some of the larger School Boards, including that for London. The lack of any organized system of secondary education, particularly in its lower stages, has resulted in the void being filled by what are known as "higher-grade" Board Schools, which, in response to a demand for commercial education unprovided for by secondary schools, have been giving what is virtually secondary education out of the rates. The School Boards have demanded that these schools should be recognized as higher elementary schools. The Board of Education has in certain cases refused—and very properly refused—such recognition where it was not satisfied of their strictly elementary character. Hence difficulties have arisen, which some have not been slow to represent as due to a reactionary and illiberal spirit at Whitehall. They are, however, due to other and, we may hope, temporary causes, which will disappear whenever the Government will put its hand seriously to the long-neglected and urgently pressing task of organizing national education. The first step towards that end will be the creation of local authorities to deal with secondary education; and whatever representation upon those authorities may hereafter be conceded to School Boards, these bodies are not in themselves, as at present elected and constituted, suitable authorities for that purpose. We trust that, till something is done, the Board of Education will keep them in their place, and see that they mind their own business within the limits, sufficiently liberal, of the Code and the Cockerton judgment.

That judgment is being denounced in various quarters as a blow to education upon another count—viz., its effect upon the evening continuation schools in London. Even Sir Charles Elliott, who is obliged to admit that, as far as the day schools are concerned, the result is not serious to the progress of education, complains that "a grievous blow has been struck at the teaching of adults in our evening schools." But granting to the full the contention that adults who have missed their school opportunities will become better citizens if they can repair the omission; granting—what has never been denied—that some system of continuation schools, such as are compulsory in certain Continental States, is desirable to prevent much of the cost of elementary education from being wasted, why must this be done at the cost of the elementary education rate? Why should it be done gratis? We cannot agree with Sir Charles Elliott that to teach English to aliens, Italians, or Polish or Russian Jews, or typewriting, shorthand, bookkeeping, and French to young people in offices and shops, is or ever could be a fair charge upon funds levied for the elementary education of children. Nor will the result for genuine continuation school pupils be very serious, if it sends them back to the polytechnics, district and town classes, and other technical instruction authorities whose function it is to provide such instruction.

Child Labour

Despite earlier legislation to prevent children working in factories, there were loopholes. Some 300,000 small children worked long hours in laundries, shops etc.

England's Vast Army of Luckless Little Toilers

Morning Leader, 7 December

The Home Office and Education Department Committees, which, under the chairmanship of Mr. H. H. S. Cunynghame, made exhaustive inquiry early in the year as to the employment of children for wages during school hours, in cases which do not come under any of the existing Acts of Parliament, has just issued its report.

It was the late Mr. Hogg who two or three years ago drew attention first to the fact that hundreds of thousands of children under eleven or twelve years of age are not protected either by the Factory Acts or the Prevention of Cruelty to Children Act from being put to and kept at work for appallingly long hours.

The committee finds that 300,000 is the lowest figure at which it can put the number, and nearly half of these children have to work for over 20 hours a week in addition to their school hours, while in many instances the hours were found to be as much as 43, 52, and 73¾ hours a week.

The committee summarizes the employments under the following general headings:

Half-timers in factories	45,000
Home industrial work	15,000
In shops	100,000
Agriculture	50,000
Street sellers	25,000
Miscellaneous	15,000

They say that the worst cases of overworking of little girls they found were in the small laundries exempt from the Acts.

Of the shops, they estimate that the newsagents employ quite 40,000 schoolboys, but as a rule the work is neither hard nor long.

The worst form of shop work they found was that of the lather-boys in Barbers' shops—five hours every evening after school, fifteen hours on Saturday, and often six to eight hours on Sunday.

A Few Hours' Work Beneficial

The committee reject the view that children ought not to be permitted to work at all. They find that it is better, mentally, morally, and physically, that they should be engaged for a few hours a day.

But the committee recommended that the work should be regulated. "It seems clear," runs the report, "that the too early employment of children may injure their future capacity, and that what is gained at the commencement of life is much more than lost at a later stage.

"It would be well if a larger number of children at an early age could be introduced to the practical work of the carpenter, shoemaker, or blacksmith, even running errands or selling newspapers helps to make them alert and industrious. To teach a lad a trade and not to teach him to work is to confound theory with practice. It is the most refined cruelty to bring a child up unaccustomed to physical labour for even one solitary hour until he is 14, and then at 14 make him do a whole day's work."

The committee recommend regulation by by-laws made by the county and borough councils in all cases, except housework in the children's own homes, and in the case of street-sellers a system of licensing as a means of enforcing the regulations.

In his supplementary report the Chief Inspector of Factories and Workshops points out that in textile factories the number of children now employed under 14 years of age far outnumbers those over 14 years, while, taking all kinds of factories together, more than half of those under 14 are employed full time.

THE NEW WOMAN

The "New Woman" was beginning to reject the majestically useless and stiffly corseted dress that was fashionable. She took to bicycling with enthusiasm. But apart from teaching, office-work and the telephone switchboards, few jobs were available to her. She had no vote. Contraception was not yet socially acceptable. Most clothes had to be made at home. The sanctity of even an unhappy marriage was still unquestioned except by the avant-garde, such as Strindberg, whose searching play on the subject, "The Dance of Death," appeared in 1901.

The Duel of Sex

From the Preface to "Man and Superman" 1901-3, Bernard Shaw.

Man is no longer, like Don Juan, Victor in The Duel of Sex. Whether he has ever been may be doubted: at all events the enormous superiority of women's natural position in this matter is telling with greater and greater force.

Marriage will persist as a name attached to a general custom long after the custom itself will have altered. . . . The progressive modification of the marriage contract will be continued until it is no more onerous nor irrevocable than any ordinary commercial deed of partnership.

Lady Surgeon Will Not Resign

Sexual discrimination prevailed in business and the professions. Although women had won the right to qualify as doctors, they still met with prejudice in practice.

Morning Leader, 7 December.

The Governors of Macclesfield Infirmary yesterday held a conference respecting the resignations of six honorary surgeons in consequence of the appointment of Miss Murdoch Clarke as junior house-surgeon.

By a majority the Governors decided to ask Miss Clarke to resign, and to give her a year's salary, her resignation being the only condition upon which the honorary medical men would return to duty.

Miss Clarke said the medical men asserted this was a question of principle with them; so it was with her. She was fighting the battle of the medical women, and declined to resign. They could dismiss her.

The conference was adjourned to enable Miss Clarke to confer with her friends.

Women and the Legal Profession

The Times, 9 January.

A case of interest to the legal profession has been raised in the Court of Session, Edinburgh. Margaret Howard Strang Hall, belonging to Kiru, in the West of Scotland, applied for admission to the law agent's examination. The Court ordered the Incorporated Society of Law Agents to lodge answers to her petition if they had any; and the society in their answers stated that no lady had ever heretofore been admitted as a legal practitioner in the country, and it was a question whether women had a legal right to admission to practice as law agents—a privilege which had been hitherto confined to men. The Statutes of their society did not appear to contemplate women becoming members of the profession, but the society did not conceive it to be their interest or their duty to maintain that women ought not to be enrolled as law agents.

Continuation of the above—court hearing of the case. The Times, 31 January.

. . . Mr. Home who appeared for Miss Hall . . . contended that there was nothing in the Statutes to prevent a lady from practising law, while modern opinion opened the way to women entering public life. . . Mr. Campbell of the Incorporated Law Agents' Society pointed out that under Roman law women were excluded from practising. . . . judgment was . . . postponed.

Graphic

WITH IMPERISHABLE ELASTIC AND SUPPORTER combined. A MILLION PAIRS ALREADY SOLD.

The great advantage of this Corset is—a combination of Elastic Texture inserted at the Waist over the hip and stomach. This "Grande nouveauté" and exquisite design reduces the most portly figure to the standard of Beauty and Fashion. To avoid deception each pair is stamped DREW'S MAKE and Trade Mark. Price 10s. 6d.; in Black, 17s. 6d. To be obtained from all Drapers and Outfitters in the Kingdom. Postage, 3d. extra. Wholesale only from DREW, SON and CO., Bath, England. Two GOLD MEDALS. Two DIPLOMAS OF MERIT.

For her morning stroll, the lady of 1901 wore a dress trimmed with gold braid, an astrakan coat with chinchilla collar, and a velvet hat crowned with geraniums.

Graphic

Women Labour and Their Wages

The Times, 2 March.

A somewhat remarkable case was heard at St. Helens yesterday, when the Lancashire Moss Litter Company were summoned for employing seven women and two girls after hours. The (factory) inspector understood that some girls worked until 11 at night and 2 in the morning. The Manager said that they paid the women 1s. 2d. a day, the standard way.

Mr. Nicholl (a magistrate)—Do you mean to say that you only pay less than 1¼d. an hour to these women?

The witness—Yes. The women started work at 6.30 a.m. and on this occasion would have worked until 9 o'clock (in the evening).

Women's International Progressive Union

The Times, 12 March.

Meeting held at Hotel Windsor. The following resolutions were unanimously passed:

1. That it is desirable in the interests of science that properly qualified women should be admitted to Fellowship in the various chartered scientific societies of this country on the same terms and conditions as men.

2. . . . that women must regain the position in London local government which they held before the passing of the London Local Government Act of 1889 . . . those present pledge themselves to do all in their power to keep the question before the public and to gain support for any Bill which may be introduced at some later date.

Women's Trade Union League

The Times, 22 March.

Affiliated to the league were some 50 different Societies with a membership of some 40,000 to 50,000 women. The League did its best to maintain unions for women and to promote trade unionism among women, supplied trained minds, persons possessing the necessary knowledge and ability to travel up and down the country to promote peaceful results where a struggle was taking place. It investigated complaints and helped those who were helpless in the pursuit of legal rights and remedies. It also helped women who did not and could not belong to a union.

Brief, Bright and Sisterly

The Woman's Journal, Boston, Mass., 25 May.

A deputation of fifteen factory women came up to London from Lancashire, bringing a petition for Parliamentary suffrage signed by 29,359 women employed in the Lancashire cotton mills. Mr. T. C. Taylor, M.P. for the Radcliffe division of Lancashire, said he had heard of larger petitions, but had never seen one. It looked like a garden roller. The Lancashire lasses set forth their views in speeches that are described as " brief, bright and sisterly ". Mrs. Millicent Garrett Fawcett entertained them at dinner, and the next day Mr. Taylor presented their petition in the House of Commons, and was cheered as he carried it with difficulty to the table.

The text of the petition:

That in the opinion of your petitioners the continued denial of the franchise to women is unjust and inexpedient.

In the home their position is lowered by such an exclusion from the responsibilities of national life.

In the factory their unrepresented condition places the regulation of their work in the hands of men who are often their rivals as well as being fellow workers.

In Parliament it causes their interests to be neglected.

A Lady Publisher

Woman, 30 October.

Small-pox; its Prevention, Treatment and History is the title of the little book just published by Florence White . . . the volume is unique in being the first book published in London bearing the imprint of a lady publisher.